Theology at 16+

Edited by James Barnett

Papers from the Eleventh
Downside Symposium

EPWORTH PRESS

7162 0400 2

First published 1984
by Epworth Press
Room 195, 1 Central Buildings
Westminster, London SW1

Phototypeset by Input Typesetting Ltd
and printed in Great Britain by
Richard Clay (The Chaucer Press) Ltd
Bungay, Suffolk

Theology at 16+

Contents

The Contributors

James Barnett	Principal of the West Oxfordshire Christian Training Scheme
Christopher Butler	Auxiliary Bishop in the Diocese of Westminster
Simon Clements	Fellow of the Centre for the Study of Comprehensive Schools in the University of York
John Coulson	Senior Lecturer in Theology in the University of Bristol
Jo Gibson	Head of First Year at Stoke Newington School
Peter Hastings	Headmaster of The Trinity School, Leamington Spa
John Kent	Professor of Theology in the University of Bristol
John Macquarrie	Lady Margaret Professor of Divinity in the University of Oxford
Stephen Sykes	Van Mildert Professor Of Divinity in the University of Durham and a Canon of Durham Cathedral
Geoffrey Turner	Lecturer in Theology at Trinity and All Saints Colleges, Leeds
Brenda Watson	Director of the Farmington Institute for Christian Studies in Oxford
Kenneth Wilson	Principal of Westminster College, Oxford
Timothy Wright	Senior RS Master and a Housemaster at Ampleforth College

Acknowledgments

The Editor wishes to acknowledge with gratitude all the help and encouragement that he has received. In particular, he is grateful to John Coulson, who made the original proposal that a Symposium should be held at Downside, and to the Abbot and Community at Downside for their hospitality, encouragement and material support. He is also grateful to John Kent, who read the typescript, made useful comments, and helped in many other ways. Naturally, he is also grateful to all who gave papers, and to those who contributed to this book, as well as to those who took part in the discussion at the Symposium itself.

In addition to that, mention must certainly be made of the help, tolerance and support given by those colleagues who made possible the travelling, absences and discussion essential to a work of this kind. In the early days of the Farmington/Ampleforth Project, that meant members of the staff at Uppingham, and, sometimes, pupils who were prepared to be taught late at night, when a regular lesson was cancelled. It is sad that Coll Macdonald, who was Headmaster of Uppingham, did not live to see the fruit of this work, to which he gave encouragement and support, both material and moral.

The Editor also thanks those with whom he has worked at the Farmington Institute for Christian Studies. Their advice has always been freely given, and it has been based on experience and expertise which it would have been difficult to have found elsewhere. He is deeply cognisant of how much he has learned from the contacts, consultations and conferences in which he has participated as a result of his association with Farmington. If there has been any skill in the editing of this book, not a little of it has been gained there.

More recently, much support has been given by colleagues in Witney, and the Editor has greatly valued their friendship, while their provision of 'cover' has made possible the continuing process of meeting and discussion on which a work of this kind is based. In particular the Reverend Roland Meredith has not only tolerated, but has actually supported a somewhat unusual style of ministry!

Lastly, mention must be made of participants in the Witney Christian Training Scheme, who are people with considerable experience and knowledge in their own fields. Although, technically, they are the Editor's pupils, they have taught him a great deal about Religious

Education, which he could not have learned elsewhere, and which has been of value in finishing this work.

Witney, September 1983   James Barnett

Introduction

James Barnett

This book is the result of an ecumenical project, which started at the beginning of 1977, and whose work has been done in three stages. In the first stage, there was close cooperation between the Heads of the Religious Education Departments in an Anglican and a Catholic School. The aim was that Religious Studies should be taken more widely by A level candidates, that truly theological syllabuses should be available, and that the method and content of RE should be such as to give it a status equal to that enjoyed by other subjects in the curriculum. In the second phase, the implications of thought and practice in the wider spectrum, and particularly in the secular school, were considered, and this was related to current views about the nature and method of theology. In the third phase, this has been considered in the light of the growing interest in the religious education of adults, and the implications of what is termed 'lay theology'.

As the work has progressed, the fundamental importance of the third phase has become increasingly clear. All education in school, at any stage, and in all areas of the curriculum, must recognize the fact that those being taught will become adults. For that reason, education in school must form the foundation on which later insight and investigation will be based. In religious education this is particularly important for two reasons. First, the committed teacher is easily tempted to look for similar commitment in his pupils at the expense of thoughtful and open investigation, which will lead to later development based on a sure understanding. Secondly, experience of teaching theology to adults suggests that the imagination, which Newman regarded as essential to true religious insight, is greatly helped by a depth of knowledge and reflection on the human predicament, which can only be gained with the passage of the years.

In the first phase of the project, the immediate result of our ecumenical activity was the production of two examination syllabuses. The first was an AO level paper in Church History. This was based on a syllabus which had been taught and examined successfully since 1975. Its aim was to help those who did the course to see that, in the last 150 years or so, developments in Christian thought and theology have been commensurate with those in other disciplines. The second syllabus was at A level, and it was concerned with the theology of the Church and Sacraments. The approach marked a significant difference from what had been attempted at this level hitherto. In particular, it was intended that those who studied the syllabus should gain some insight into the cohesiveness of Christian doctrine, and the reasons for its development. A further aim was that this would give a good insight into the nature and scope of theology as a whole.

An important aspect of our syllabus was that it entailed a thematic method of study. Candidates were required to study important aspects of Christian development from the earliest times to the present day. They were also required to know something of Christian antecedents, and of the inter-testamental period, so as to be able properly to understand the meaning and nature of early Christian vocabulary. Set texts were prescribed from both the Bible and other Christian writing, and they were chosen and studied in such a way as to demonstrate the nature and development of the appropriate topic, rather than as a study of a book or books.

This led to a more complete view of the interrelationship of different parts of the New Testament than has often been the case. Moreover, the application of this method of study to the extra-biblical material meant that, within the obvious limitation of a syllabus at this level, as complete a view as possible of theological development was made available to those who studied the syllabus. All this pointed to fundamental questions about the nature of religious education, and its relationship to the general development of young people.

Traditionally in the church, and until recently in many schools, religious teaching was given by a deductive method. Its purest form is catechesis, which has often been done as a process of question and answer. The principle is that biblical precepts, or the teaching of the church, are specifically identified and applied generally to life. In a secular age like our own, and at a time when people are expected to question and test what they are taught, this application of a received tradition is unlikely to be acceptable. Our aim, therefore, was to help young people to see the importance of man's spiritual experience by as rigorous an examination of doctrine as is possible at this level. In that way we hoped that they would think seriously not only about doctrine but also about the importance to its adherents of the experience on which it is based.

It became clear that, in dealing with the principle of academic rigour we were concerned with the educational rather than the 'ecclesiastical' justification for RE. If our work were to be really valuable, the principle would have to be tested in terms of its applicability to schools of all types. This demanded consideration of current thought about theological method in the university, and about its implications for the teaching of young people in school. The rich diversity of the educational system meant that we would be helped by the successful experience of people who have worked in different types of school.

That led to the second stage of our project, where we were drawn into the wider debate. It became clear that we would have to consider current practice in the secular school, and the appropriateness of what we were doing to that situation. In particular, there were the implications of what is loosely termed 'indoctrination', since, if our syllabus were to have a proper standing in the academic timetable, it would have to be capable of being taught in such a way as not to make improper assumptions about the prior beliefs of the pupils involved.

In this respect, our first aim, which was concerned with making available for A level candidates truly theological syllabuses, the standard of which was equal to that of other subjects, was particularly appropriate as a starting point. It was shared with other teachers, who advocated syllabuses with a content markedly different from our own, but who, like us, sought to help young people to see that religious insights and experience merit serious consideration. The Theology Department of the Trinity School in Leamington Spa has done some very interesting work in this area. A voluntary aided comprehensive school, in which many pupils share the attitudes of the industrial Midlands, it has been remarkably successful in enabling them to see the importance of theology as they seek to make sense of their experience of the world, as of religion and of the way in which they relate to each other. The paper by Peter Hastings and Geoffrey Turner considers some aspects of this work.

At this stage we were particularly fortunate in being able to draw on the expertise of people involved in the current debate at the highest level in the university, on the experience of others who had been involved in the training of teachers and in examination work, and on the experience of teachers whose work had been in the secular milieu, against the background of which our work would have to be tested if its value were to be clearly seen and understood. This led to a symposium at Downside, at which papers representative of the whole situation were given, and a good number of which form the basis of this book.

A particularly interesting feature of this stage of the work is shown by the contribution of the Deputy Head of Woodberry Down Comprehensive School, Simon Clements, and Jo Gibson, a former Head of RE in the same school. Both of them see Religious Education in terms of a search or quest for truth, where the starting point is the experience of the pupil, and where, as a consequence, the context in which he lives is of fundamental importance. For Simon Clements, that context is the inner city, and an urban experience, the nature of which even the more recent of our ancestors cannot have foreseen. In such a situation, theology, like any other academic study must be seen to work if it is to have value; if this is to be done well, most of what Simon Clements terms 'the baggage of the past' will have to be reassessed. The search which this entails must be conducted at first hand, yet it is often difficult to have first hand experience even of what is known. An example of this is disablement.

Jo Gibson, whose concern had centred on the RE syllabus as a specific area within the curriculum as a whole, had succeeded in establishing the importance of RE in the eyes of both pupils and parents with a syllabus very different from our own. Her method was an inductive one, which took as its starting point such experiences as birth, puberty, marriage and death. By looking at what the Great World Faiths found in the vicinity of the school said about inevitable first-hand experience, she was employing a method which was almost the direct opposite of the one traditionally employed by the Christian churches, and implicitly called in question by our syllabus.

The obvious success of this method at Woodberry Down demonstrates its applicability to that situation. Where pupils were drawn from so wide a variety of backgrounds, it avoided the making of assumptions not only about what pupils believe, but also about the way in which they had been affected by cultural influences, which are at one remove from religion. One aspect of its value lay in the way in which it helped prejudiced and sometimes inarticulate young people to understand better those with whom they shared a classroom. This demonstrated a social value in addition to the more specific application of the syllabus to religious insight and experience, which was part of the school's curricular responsibility.

It became apparent, therefore, that in practice, as well as in theory, our first aim of helping the young to take seriously the religious experience of man, could be achieved by syllabuses whose content was fundamentally different. In admittedly different milieux both types of syllabus pointed to the importance both of religion and of the experience on which it is based. Both syllabuses also provided an educational justification which raised questions about traditional and often current practice in the churches. Moreover, though we had succeeded in demonstrating that religion is not uninteresting, and merits serious consideration, we had done nothing to initiate our pupils into the fullness of religious experience or practice, although it was to be hoped, expected, and was subsequently demonstrated in experience, that the believers among our pupils were helped in the quest in which they were already engaged.

This raised important issues concerned with the completion and fulfilment of RE, and about the nature of theology. We all saw religious education as being concerned with the search or quest, and this was in accord with the way in which theology and the church's understanding of her ministry are more tentative today than they were in the past. Nevertheless, there were two real difficulties. First, the inductive approach, based on experience, need not lead to a serious investigation of religion, much less to a particular faith. It followed that, in this area, so-called 'life stances' like Marxism or humanism could obstruct the serious investigation of spiritual understanding. It is the special nature of that understanding which is the object of truly religious education, and which gives it its right to a place in the school curriculum. Secondly, there was a danger that the investigation of religion by people who are, as yet, not religious, might be done at second or third hand, rather than as something in which young people were personally involved.

The implications of this were clarified by those involved in the study of theology in a university setting. This is particularly demonstrated by a comparison of the papers by Stephen Sykes and John Coulson. For John Coulson experience is essential to the proper understanding of theology. On the one hand he has pointed to the growth of interconfessional theology. By implication, he has also pointed to the acceptance by different Christian traditions of the nature of a discipline in the practice of which they now share in a way in which they did not do so twenty years ago. On the other hand, he has pointed to the growth of lay theology, which suggests the development of what he terms the old pastoral systematic theology to a theology 'of the foundations'. The standpoint of the practitioner may be confessional or secular, but it is clear that this theology must be done in the university, since that is the creative centre of our culture. In particular, the university makes possible dialogue with other disciplines, of which the study of literature is an example, so that the contextual relevance, and the connection of theology with experience may be appreciated.

For John Coulson, as for Stephen Sykes, the diversity of areas of study, or even of disciplines, on which theology depends, poses difficulties. For John Coulson, theology is a third order discipline, whose function is to inform second order disciplines, which may, like philosophy, history or exegesis, be part of theology itself. In a society with no agreed metaphysic, and in a climate of thought where there is little agreement about which discipline is prior to others in theology, it becomes necessary to follow Rahner to go beneath theology to its foundation in experience, and so to encounter the darkness of God.

This paper points to the regulative function of theology, in the confessional milieu, and exemplifies this with the Theology of the Church and Sacraments Syllabus. Where assessment is based on adequacy of argument, an examinable syllabus in the confessional school has an essential function in harmonizing and bringing into equilibrium the doctrines, devotions and acts of Christianity which must be done in each generation. The practice of the syllabus bears this out.

Nevertheless there are other factors. John Coulson considers the secular school where the problem is not about what we believe, but about whether we need to believe anything, or to have beliefs in common. On the one hand this leads him to support Jo Gibson's method; on the other hand, in comparing school and university, he is caught in the difficulty of reconciling faith and facts. This is exemplified by Matthew Arnold's describing himself as living between two worlds,

'one dead, the other powerless to be born'.

He can live neither without Christianity, nor with it as it is.

Here Stephen Sykes' paper, which actually makes a less direct attempt to come to terms with the problem of the secular school, comes to the rescue. Like John Coulson, Stephen Sykes is concerned with the 'components' of theology, or the areas of study which it comprises. Now, however, the problem is less one of disparity of method than of lack of cohesiveness in the English tradition of theology. On the one hand, this is shown in the way in which the various aspects of theology with an Anglican heritage in the secular university do not hang together. This is exemplified by the syllabus at Cambridge in the late fifties. On the other hand, if a paper on the History of Christian Doctrine to AD 451 could give students the idea that christological disagreement came to an end with the Council of Chalcedon, the 1970 reform of the Cambridge Tripos enables theologians to 'plunder Forsyth, Rahner and Pannenberg for christological opinions, unencumbered by any instruction in Athanasius, Ne Nestorius or Cyril'.

This implies the need for a complete theology which recognizes the ecclesial nature of the European tradition. The need is exemplified with reference to Lonergan, and Stephen Sykes places much emphasis on the need for dialectic, which is lacking in the English tradition. That need points to the paper on the Theology of the Church and Sacraments, with which the project began. This paper, which was aimed at giving pupils some understanding of the scope and nature of theology, was also aimed at giving them a knowledge of Christian development in such a way that they could see something of the nature and reason for disagreement within Christianity as a whole. In that way, those who have done the paper have been able to see that man's experience of God can, and will, sustain serious debate and discussion. The importance of this is not only that it gives an honest account of denominational differences, but also that it points to the way in which religion requires serious consideration. It is hoped that the method developed in this paper, and the syllabus based on it, may be extended to include distinctive aspects of the theology of as many Christian traditions as possible.

In the third phase of the work, the importance of all this is seen in perspective. Earlier in the life of the project, there was a good deal of discussion about whether the norm for RE should be sought in the sixth form or earlier. Discussion tended to bring us back to the importance of the sixth form on the ground that this was the stage when people began to ask the sort of question about justice, suffering, or the meaning of life, which is integral to the religious quest. In other words, we began to see that a complete theology demanded not only that people should reflect on experience at first hand, but also that they should have such a maturity of outlook as to be able to supplement observation with serious reflection.

For the first part, this obviously pointed to the common nature of much human experience. Here the model of the common or truly comprehensive school, representative of society at large, in which all must live, was clearly important. This did not meet the objection, stated earlier, however, that experience need not point to religion in general or to Christianity in particular. At this point we were faced with the question of how one should teach a balanced theology. This meant that we had not only to endeavour to demonstrate the scope and nature of the discipline within an A level syllabus and the time available for teaching it, but also to consider the requirement that people should understand the relative importance of the different elements involved.

In this the editor has been particularly helped by his experience in teaching theology to adults, whose experience in life is as disparate as their age. For these people, the academic stimulus of investigating the interrelationship of different aspects of Christian doctrine is given contextual relevance by their endeavour to live the Christian life. Spiritual experience, together with having striven in prayer and its difficulties, is coupled with having lived for a sufficient number of years to have a background of mature and profound reflection on the human predicament. At the same time, adults tend to have specialized knowledge either in the formal sense, or from having worked in a particular field, and this knowledge both informs and is informed by theological reflection. This gives a quality to their work which is not available to young people. For the latter, the twofold observation of the system of doctrine and the nature of life can only be made complete by a reflection on experience which is fed by time and based on imagination.

This gives legitimacy to the question of whether there is any point in teaching RE in school, raised by John Kent's paper. It also points to the need for a balanced theology, and the difficulty of providing that balance for people whose experience is necessarily limited. First, it is clear that a good deal of what is done in school must be preparatory, or, in Newman's terms, a propaedeutic activity, since the experience of young people in those areas with which religion is concerned is, in the great majority of cases, too incomplete for them to have a first-hand knowledge of the depth of human spiritual awareness. Secondly, it follows from this lack of first-hand knowledge that theology in school will often be incomplete and so unbalanced.

These two factors, together with inevitable differences of attitude to theology, religion and education among the contributors, added greatly to the interest of the editorial task. Indeed, from a very early stage in the preparation, which was to result in this book, we were concerned with the question of the most appropriate title. On the one hand, the syllabuses which we had developed, and the form which our work had taken, pointed to the appropriateness of *Theology at 16+*. On the other hand, our concern with the needs and practice of the secular school, and our recognition of the appropriateness of syllabuses based on Religious Studies in schools like Woodberry Down, caused us to pay attention to the implications of those things, and to consider a rival claimant, *Christian Studies at 16+*, which would have given explicit recognition to the difficulties of doing theology without first-hand knowledge or commitment.

Moreover, the experience of Woodberry Down pointed to the needs of the significant number of pupils in our schools, whose backgrounds represent non-European culture and a variety of religious traditions. Any educational philosophy must take account of this, and the experience gained in places with a multi-faith tradition must be available to all. By the same token, those responsible for religious education in places with a small immigrant population should acquaint themselves with the changes brought about elsewhere if their work is really to prepare young people for the future.

In this area there are two very important issues. First there is the problem of particularism, when one faith affirms what another equally specifically denies. For example, the incarnation, which is blasphemy to the Jews and folly to the Greeks, poses particular difficulty for the Muslim. At the same time, it provides both the context and the material for serious investigation of the kind that may lead to a degree of mutual understanding, which would not otherwise be attained. It follows that, as in any other subject, truly satisfactory teaching requires awareness of divergent views, not all of which are part of the experience of those being taught. In this respect, the needs of the pluralist society may serve to modify the method of RE in schools where the difficulties which it raises are not so immediately apparent.

This leads to the second point. If teaching enables people of different outlooks to take seriously the views of others, it must of necessity demonstrate the importance and value of the material being studied. One of the ways in which this may be done entails the investigation of experience common to all people, so as to help the young to see the relationship and relevance of religion to their experience of life. That accounts for the importance of the rites of passage in syllabuses used by teachers in schools like Jo Gibson's. Such experience as birth, puberty, marriage and death are shared by everyone, and their importance is obvious. It is also particularly easy to see how serious religious reflection has been based on these things.

Jo Gibson's syllabus, therefore, represents work, the importance of which includes the way in which it may help people to take seriously, and to reflect upon outlooks other than their own. If it is relevant to the plural and multi-faith society, it is also relevant to the secular one, since it may help people with a materialist outlook to regard the religious one as being worthy of consideration. The selection of material from Jo Gibson's syllabus has been made with this in mind. That material shows how both rites of passage and the cycle of the seasons may form the content of a syllabus which demonstrates the importance of religion and the search for meaning and purpose on which it is based. It also shows their relevance to first-hand experience.

The importance of these matters should not be obscured by the editor's choice of the title *Theology at 16+*. That choice was governed by two things. First there was the conviction that, as an educaton which ignores the spiritual experience of man is *ipso facto* defective, so religious education should supply as good an understanding as possible of the foundations on which adult insights may, eventually, be built. Secondly, careful reading showed how this aim is common to the papers in this book, despite their apparent divergence of outlook, a matter described earlier in the introduction, and now requiring further amplification.

This underlying unity is best described in relation to the terms of reference of theology, and the way in which those terms of reference are understood by the different contributors. At first sight, the differences of approach to the study of theology described by John Coulson and Stephen Sykes are mirrored by those whose contributions are based on experience and practice in the classroom. Thus the support explicitly given by John Coulson to a method of religious education based on the life experience of the pupil may be compared to the *Theology of the Church and Sacraments* syllabus, with its clear affinity to the practice of theology as an ecclesial discipline. Such a distinction, which may be closely connected with the debate about the relative merits of Religious Studies and so-called 'Christian' syllabuses, is, however, misleadingly trite.

In this respect, the import of the papers in this book is that the relationship between religious education in the secular school and the best of what is being done in a denominational setting needs to be more clearly defined than has often been the case. That is because there are necessary limitations in the terms of reference of young people from different backgrounds, which are no less important than the stated aims or objectives of religious education. This can be seen even in the comparison of the papers by Jo Gibson and Simon Clements, both of which were written from within the same milieu. For Jo Gibson as a head of department, the task was to produce a syllabus which would interest and stimulate children whose secular concern was concentrated on earning, buying and enjoyment, and whose dismissal of the religious quest of mankind made their interpretation of life and experience more difficult than it need have been. For Simon Clements, however, theology must be done 'on the street'. By that he means that it must take account of the whole milieu in which the student lives and works, which includes the range of problems and experience in which the school administrator has, of necessity, to share. It is obvious that, in such a setting, theology cannot be regarded as an ecclesial discipline.

Careful reading of the papers in the book suggests that, in the very different milieu of the independent school, the same principles apply. Here, as in the secular school, the context in which theology is studied is of basic importance. For Timothy Wright at Ampleforth, an important part of the context of the search, and therefore of its terms of reference, is supplied by the monastic community. This has a considerable influence on the way in which theology is studied, even though it is different from the one supplied by the streets of Hackney. For James Barnett, the same principles produced a slightly different problem. Although few, if any, pupils at Uppingham choose the school for its 'Anglican' tradition, their home backgrounds, and the independent preparatory school mean that, for the great majority of the pupils, the language of religion is made up of Christian vocabulary, even if that vocabulary is imperfectly understood. It follows that, in both contexts, a serious study of Christian teaching, and of the vocabulary on which it is based, is possible. The appropriateness of this method as a basis on which to develop an understanding of the nature of religion in the confessional or in the 'secular Anglican' school serves, therefore, to support rather than to question the stress laid by Jo Gibson on the importance of its context to the study of theology.

Indeed, John Macquarrie points to the same principle *within* the Christian tradition when he writes of 'indigenous theology', of which black theology is an example. At another – and earlier – point in his paper, he deals with the question of whether an atheist can properly be said to be a serious student of theology. His view that, although this study is not possible for the atheist, it can be performed by the sympathetic agnostic points to the value of what Jo Gibson did at Woodberry Down. She enabled people with neither the awareness nor the vocabulary of true religion to be awakened to issues that might easily have been avoided. Children could explore more fully, and explain more deeply, their own thoughts and feelings, and, by implication, see the importance of theology.

If this last point also expresses the aims, and one hopes the results of the work done by Timothy Wright and James Barnett, to which reference was made earlier, it points to three additional conclusions. First, the model for religious education anywhere may be found in the best of what is done in the secular school. If, within the context of that experience, young people may be helped to begin a lifelong reflection on what are termed 'ultimate issues', and if they can be given some of the vocabulary with which to do that, and to see its importance, religious education will have justified its place in the curriculum. Secondly, however, although an education which ignores the spiritual experience of man is defective, the limitations imposed by the school milieu must raise serious questions about the necessary incompleteness of religious education. This leads to the third point, which is concerned with the personal quality and ability of the teacher. No small part of the reason for Jo Gibson's success was concerned with the way in which, by broadening the horizons of her pupils, she broke down their prejudices and awakened their interest.

In this area, Kenneth Wilson's paper is helpful. It points to the theme of the book. Writing from the standpoint of one concerned with Christian theology, he describes religion as an adult activity, and points to the way in which, that notwithstanding, religious education in schools must be taught in such a way as not to have to be unlearned. To theologize is to enquire, and this entails enquiry about the world and life, as well as about God. If this is to be properly done, then RE must take account of what is being done in other areas of the curriculum. Thus the last paper of the symposium is linked, by the breadth of its terms of reference, to Simon Clements' theological interpretation of many aspects of life in the inner city. This requires in the teacher a quality of method and approach, if possible a breadth of experience, and certainly a capacity for personal growth, of which his training must take full account, and which it must endeavour to foster.

Thus the choice of 'theology' for the title of our book is justified. The search or quest, the importance of which all must accept, should be seen in relation to the context in which it takes place, and the experience which that context provides. It must also include an adequate vocabulary. Although the former, supplied by life, and the latter, based on religious systems, are not always the same, the task of the teacher of RE is to point young people, despite the limited nature of their experience, to a quest which can be neither complete in this world, nor indefinitely postponed. The enquiry which this entails is one in which, in the nature of the case, each should be involved, and yet from which each must be passionately detached, if it is to be undertaken with the rigour which produces real insight.

Although syllabuses will be developed, and discussion of their content will continue, the editor hopes that, by its community of purpose, apparent diversity of outlook notwithstanding, this volume will make a real contribution to the continuing debate.

The papers of this book are written by people whose range of experience and outlook should help the reader to see both what is being done, and how current practice may be related to the more specific needs of different schools. The opening and closing papers are also concerned with the way in which theology must be related to life as a whole.

1. Simon Clements was Deputy Head of Woodberry Down Comprehensive School in Hackney. He considers the place of Religious

Education in School in relation to both the formal curriculum and the whole life of the school community. Theology whose quality of method is so good as to enable religious education to justify itself should be done 'on the street'. In this way it may be for all people in the common school. The finest ideas are of interest to all, but they are best understood in a freedom more redolent of the infant than the secondary school. Moreover, we must see knowledge as unified, and religion is a unifying factor in school.

This is followed by four papers from contributors with considerable experience of teaching RE in different milieux. They should be considered together. Moreover, the last two papers of the four – those by Timothy Wright and James Barnett – should be seen as one contribution, because they describe ecumenical cooperation which led to the development of common syllabuses.

The content of Jo Gibson's paper is particularly relevant to the secular and multi-cultural society of some of our large cities, and particular attention should be paid to the importance, in her work, of teaching about rites of passage. The obvious success of the content and method of what was done in her school is demonstrated by the way in which it helped her pupils to give serious thought to what they had been ready to dismiss. *Mutatis mutandis*, this work should be of use to practising teachers elsewhere.

The second of the papers, by Peter Hastings and Geoffrey Turner, which also reflects the comprehensive school, was written as a result of their contribution to our Downside meeting. In many respects, Leamington Spa is part of the industrial Midlands, and it became clear in discussion that any examination of RE would be incomplete if it did not consider the place of the maintained or voluntary aided confessional school working in a secular milieu. Jo Gibson's work, which enabled people to see how religious vocabulary in the broader sense could help them to face issues, the real import of which might otherwise have been missed, must be compared with a similar exercise based on a more predominantly Christian vocabulary. Although Leamington Spa contains a smaller 'cultural mix' than Hackney, and although a confessional school is, to an important extent, selective, this method of RE is no less helpful to the pupils involved than the methods described in the other papers by teachers.

Consideration is given to the relationship of theology to the work of the church by the comparison of the ways in which an ecclesial theology was taught in a monastic setting and in the (more secular) one of an Anglican Public School. In the former there is an element of rigorous examination of the received tradition of Christian Doctrine, which was less prominent in James Barnett's more secular experience. In the latter case, the need was to help young people to see that Christian experience, and the teaching based on it, merited serious consideration. This should be compared with Jo Gibson's work, which was concerned with the common needs of a plural and secular society. It should be contrasted with the development of the A/O level syllabus at Ampleforth to include the study of spirituality, as well as the Modern Church History with which it began.

2. Jo Gibson writes about the need to make young people 'religiate', which is the theological equivalent of 'literate' and 'numerate'. She considers the implications of different backgrounds and milieux, and the nature of religious education where the cultural and religious outlook of the pupils is drawn from a number of traditions. She also considers respectable RE for the non-academic pupil.

3. Peter Hastings and Geoffrey Turner consider the role of the confessional school in society at large. Its function is to serve the needs of the pupil, and this is of more importance than that of the church. That function entails an active criticism of a society which includes the church. It also means that young people must be helped to examine their personal religious experience, since such examination helps in the later adult act of affirmation. Like James Barnett, they are concerned to help pupils to think hard about Christianity and their own attitude to it.

4. This may be contrasted with the monastic school, exemplified by Ampleforth. Timothy Wright speaks of the nature of faith, and the place of the teacher's commitment in helping to foster the faith of his pupils. He also considers the development of RE in the school since the Second Vatican Council.

5. James Barnett has taught craft apprentices in a technical college, and was on the staff of Hutton Grammar School, before he went to Uppingham. He is currently engaged, inter alia, in teaching theology to adults in West Oxfordshire. He suggests that religious education in Anglican Independent Schools since the war has been neither theological nor catechetical, and he uses his work at Uppingham to point to the way in which, in many schools, Christian theology may supply a proper basis for RE. His experience suggests that the work which he has done with Timothy Wright has relevance and effectiveness in many situations.

This raises issues both of who will teach the subject, and of how it will be assessed. In practical terms, the availability of suitably qualified teachers must be considered, and this must be seen in relation to currently available examinations, and likely or desirable development.

6. Brenda Watson has experience of training teachers, and has done a good deal of work on A level syllabuses. After consideration of the need for properly trained teachers, and of the adequacy or otherwise of the present provision in that respect, she raises questions about the appropriateness of the examination system. In particular, after looking at a number of methods of assessment, she suggests that the greater part of the lesson time available in school should be used in such a way as to make in-depth enquiry and investigation an integral part of the course. She connects this with consideration of the appropriateness of theology to the school. She also considers the importance of the teacher's personality to good education.

The method employed by the teacher is also related to work currently being done in the University, since, if teachers are to prepare young people to make adult judgments about the issues involved, they must take account of what is being done at that level. The fact that these papers, like the ones written by teachers, reflect certain differences of emphasis, demonstrates their relevance to syllabus construction based on an understanding of current theological debate.

7. John Kent starts by considering the change which has come over religious education in recent years, and looks at both the reasons for that change, and the difficulties involved in more traditional methods. In doing this, he examines the views of the 'modern masters', and the difficulties of honest teaching, which both respects the right of the individual to the essential activity of making up his own mind, and examines the difficulty of giving real meaning to theological language and vocabulary in a secular milieu. In raising questions about the appropriateness of religious education in the school, he points to the adult practice and outlook which are essential to the debate in the university.

This directs attention to the question raised earlier in the introduction, which is developed by Stephen Sykes and John Coulson.

8. John Coulson, working in the same University, develops John Kent's question about the appropriateness and intelligibility of Christian language to the secular milieu. While accepting the appropriateness of theology to the confessional school, he points to the importance of experience, and its place as a starting point in the secular world.

9. Stephen Sykes, on the other hand, in arguing for the ecclesial nature of theology, points to the importance of actual knowledge as a basis from which young people may proceed to their own investigation. At the same time, he recognizes the need for RE to cater for an entire population, and to take account of Western Youth Culture. He is

anxious that the study of dialectic should exhibit the debate within Christianity, by which many of its different aspects have been affected.

This makes essential the treatment of the topics covered by the next two papers. Here the relationship of theology to the church, religious belief and experience is considered. In terms of the book as a whole, these papers look at some of the issues which had to be faced earlier by the practising teacher. It is intended that these papers should help the reader to understand not only some of the issues involved in teaching religious education well in the confessional school, but also that they should help people in all types of school better to understand the way in which people use language to explain their belief. The importance of this is self-evident.

10. Christopher Butler examines the relationship between theology and doctrine in the light of teaching about the authority of the church. He considers the relative primacy of theology and doctrine, and the relationship of theologians to the pope and bishops. In saying that theology is chronically unofficial, he also says that it should be respected. This is a Roman Catholic position, but he draws attention to the need to take seriously the theology of Vatican II and its implications for ecumenism.

11. John Macquarrie considers the nature of theology and religion. He questions whether there can be value-free knowledge, and applies this to the Oxford tradition of theology. In doing so, he picks up an important aspect of Stephen Sykes's paper. He also draws attention to the difference between theology and religious belief, and so to an issue which implicitly underlies the Theology of the Church and Sacraments syllabus. There is an important respect in which theology enables people to enquire further about the language in which they explain their belief. This raises the question of whether the non-believer can study theology, and so of the relationship of theology, religion and ideology, which is essential to a complete examination of RE today.

12. Finally, Kenneth Wilson, who is Principal of Westminster College, Oxford, considers the way in which the foundations of theological enquiry may be laid down for the young. In particular, he is concerned that the training of teachers should enable them to introduce young people, as far as is possible, to the nature of adult insights about religion and spirituality. In terms of the more general implications of this, a sufficient number of students at his college are already reading theology for everyone in the college, regardless of their specialized fields, to have close contact with a theologian during his time at Westminster.

1 Setting the Scene: Charting the Landscape
Simon Clements

I have in mind two titles for this paper: 'What's Hecuba to him, or he to Hecuba' and 'Notes to the hurrying Man', from Brian Patten's poems. Hecuba is what we teach the children, and hurrying is personal.

In being asked to open this symposium, I certainly feel a 'rogue and peasant slave' when faced with such a company. I feel that my only base for authority is the running I do, the thinking on the hoof, 'making oneself a place in that sad traffic you call a world', because I can assure you that this is no learned theological paper recollected in tranquillity, but thoughts gasped between family life and school. The hurrying means that I tend to address my family as if they are the lower school assembly, and, in moments of exhaustion, I am likely to call naughty and recalcitrant pupils 'darling' or 'love'. Either the interchangeability is a sign of imminent breakdown, or it is an aspect of continuity between family and school.

The Hecuba bit has always struck me as a teacher; again I'm standing on the staircase, watching the pupils hurrying, no 'creeping like a snail unwillingly to school' as they struggle towards their classrooms. 'What's Geology to him, or she to Theology,' I wonder; for so much of the curriculum seems to be *ours*, our invention, academic, bourgeois, adult. Someone once said that this world or society is intended for middle-aged, middle-class, childless white males, and that the rest of us are a nuisance. Many of our lessons, I sometimes feel, are as remote as Hecuba, and yet so many children's engagements with their Hecubas see them 'drown their stage with tears'.

I want to suggest that Hecuba is for all people, just as Hamlet and the common player were on the same mortal earth, striving with the same concerns and similar capacities. Our Hecuba is theology and the cultural tradition, and I suggest that there cannot be one theology and tradition for Hamlet and another for the player. Our subject is one, its study is the same at any level, and to any audience.

This is very important in school, because we are committed to the avoidance of a popular anti-intellectualism and to reminding ourselves, with Gerald Priestland, that 'Greece is part of our souls' (*The Listener*, 24 September 1981). The important thing is that we should avoid having two versions of any subject, one for the secondary moderns, and another, respectable one for the academic children. In abandoning the tripartite system, we turned our backs on the fragmentation of knowledge. Yet I suspect that, at the time, no one quite guessed how much the principle of the comprehensive school would challenge the curriculum. At first the fragmentation continued through streaming, but now we are concerned to define a subject in such a way that it relates meaningfully to pupils, while also reflecting its central traditions. In school, we have come to recognize that the study of a subject must combine both the encounter with received tradition, and the study of what others have said, together with a serious recognition of adolescent questions, concerns and search for meaning.[1] Like John Berger's artist, the adolescent in school or university is part of the 'renewing of the tradition in which he works, making new the language he inherits'. The teacher must, therefore, construct syllabuses which leave pupils to formulate their own understanding and response, for there are two versions or aspects of any subject; *our* curriculum and *theirs*. Although Hecuba is one, the educated Hamlet watched a contemporary player re-engage with the old story.

There is another point about that scene; its setting. The milieu was a corrupt court, where a distracted prince was working with travelling players in a cobbled courtyard. The sense of Hecuba grew out of a particular condition. It reminds me of the imagery and setting, the sense of the open road and the hurry, which Passolini used in his film *The Gospel according to St Matthew*, where his Christ was always watching, always moving, doing his thinking and teaching on the move, in the fields, on the road, in an atmosphere of urgency, responding to his times.

As the common player can engage with Hecuba, so we should take heart about the place of theology or religious studies in education. Each subject has to justify itself, and I do not think that theology has more difficulty than other subjects. It is certainly true in our school that religious studies need not run into any more problems of resistance than Spanish or needlework for boys, or physical education, especially at the age when pupils are making final choices of subjects for their last period of schooling. The problems facing religious studies are the same as those facing other subjects. The issues in school are about styles of teaching, interest, intellectual excitement, the imagination, creative response, personal growth – all those things for which we teach, whatever our subject. In all areas of the curriculum, it is the quality of *method* that matters. I occasionally say 'Child, it doesn't matter what the subject is, I'm concerned to teach you punctuality, good habits of personal organization, the practice of attentive listening, and the ability to observe; today we happen to be doing that through the study of those pebbles on the beach!'

The issue of method is fundamental to any discussion of education, not as a technique, but as an approach: it is that necessary openness to the questions and development of the child and adolescent as he thinks critically about the subject being taught. I call it the pastoral element in the academic process. It has great power to clarify and affect the content of a subject.

Setting the scene

As Hecuba is for all, in this paper I wish to consider 'theology on the streets' responding to its times, and, in particular, the place of theology in school. For that reason, I shall deliberately look at the whole experience of a child before the sixth form because I think that the years of schooling are interdependent. I shall consider the secular school alone, because I think that it simplifies the argument I wish to mount, which is that the proper study of religious questions at any age is theological.

If we get this theology right in the secular uncommitted, undenominational school, perhaps we are saying more about the essence of theology in education than can be said if it is practised only in a believing community.[2] In the secular school, theology simply cannot be an ecclesial discipline alone, and the claim of the market place as a forum for theology must be recognized. Donald Reeves, Rector of St James, Piccadilly, and Director of the Urban Ministry Project, put it this way in a letter to *The Listener* (8 October 1981):

Doing this theology – on the streets, as opposed to in the study – creates, at last, an opportunity for clergy and their congregations to appropriate their faith. The retreat of the theologians to university faculties (there are, of course, some distinguished exceptions) has been one of the many factors in contributing to the portrait of the average Christian as ignorant, confused and generally inarticulate.

Bring theology out of the closet, and once again it might, just

might, generate the poetry and passion proper to its material and its
task.

I suggest that what is here true for theology is true also for other
subjects in the school curriculum, and that the relationship between
university and laity touched on here would be recognized by many of
us in schools, who are worried about the way in which some universities
misread the language and minds of adolescents as a result of the
examiners' control of criteria for O and A levels.

In fact, the secular or non-selective comprehensive school is a historic
institution of our times, which has a certain affinity with the monastic
movement of the eighth century. This embodiment of ideas and form
in exact relationship is reflected by A. N. Whitehead, who noticed that
the genius of the Benedictine movement was the way in which it had
the ability to embody high ideals in an institutional form. I have often
thought that the comprehensive school is similar. The ideal or principle
is that education is for all people, 'whether Jew or gentile, man or
woman, bondman or free', and that presupposes that knowledge and
human wisdom shall be available to be shared by all people regardless
of circumstance or ability. It is a democratic expression: the prince can
learn with the strolling players. There is little else that dares such an
all-embracing purpose in which its principles affect every detail of its
structure and its day. Selective schools are not that, they are partial
because they have chosen, with clear reason, to do a particular task in
a particular way.

When a pupil falls foul in a comprehensive school, there is virtually
nowhere else to go. So we have to live and soldier on with people as
they are, not unlike the church. I say this because I think that it is a
principle which is often forgotten; certainly it is forgotten by the media
and the press, who are quick to pick on the faults of the comprehensive
school. If we had abandoned monasticism after twenty-five years
because there had been some truancy in the cloister, or illegible
manuscripts, history would have declared the decision as premature,
and we would have been the poorer. But twenty-five years is, after all,
the time during which the comprehensive movement has been under
way. Education for all is only 110 years old, and education for all
adolescents is only some fifty years old. We are still attempting to
understand the task, let alone find the right means and forms for meeting
the needs. The challenge for university and school is to find the
curriculum for the common school, and, in return, we can expect some
surprising implications for each subject.

One form of meeting the need of pupils which arises out of the common school is the idea of examinations which are course-based. These exams establish that the pupils, with their teachers, will have a considerable influence on both the content and form of the curriculum. The JMB has now pioneered an entirely course-based O level English exam, which includes the study of texts. This represents a major breakthrough, because we have an exam which recognizes that we should examine fifteen-year-olds at their point of personal development. In other words, it examines *them* in *their* use of *their* language, rather than by the criteria of adulthood alone. I am not talking about accuracy here, but about the gestation of adequate language. Course based exams, built upon, and reflecting the development of pupils, mirror good syllabuses developed out of a teacher's first-hand interest and exploration. I suggest that if this is relevant for English, it is also relevant for theology which must balance its own language with 'the language of search' as coming from the adolescent. Indeed, in this symposium, any consideration of a theological curriculum for schools *must* consider the new developments in method and organization with which teachers are involved.

The JMB highlights another important aspect: the relationship of the university, sixth form and school. Yet we are in for a period of discontinuity with the sixth forms being hived off, and I am worried by the possibility of a disjointed community of knowledge if the new approaches of both school and university are not influencing and listening to one another. It could mean that the continuity of teaching between thirteen- and seventeen-year-olds will be threatened, and, although syllabuses can help, experience is what matters – the experience of discovering that a poem or idea that is being discussed with a sixth form can also go down well with a third form and vice-versa. Despite the change in maturity which affects the nature of the questions and concerns of the young, the task of the teacher is the same, and this demands contact with the whole age range if his perception of the possibilities is not to be lost.

I have said that these are early years for the comprehensive schools. One of the tragedies of present educational policy is the rift between local authority, maintained and private independent schools. There seems to be so little contact, so little mutual discussion of common ideas. Yet I believe that we have something to learn from each other. Parents are being torn apart, trying to find answers and reassurance, which it is difficult to give. The community of education is suffering from this division, so I hope very much that this symposium may be seen as one exercise of a coming together for the benefit of all children.

Back to the secular secondary school. We should not go far into this symposium without at least referring to the law about compulsory religious education.

What actually happens

The normal practice with RS, as with all other subjects, is that it is compulsory for the first three years, 11 to 14. Then, in the fourth year, pupils choose about half their curriculum. It is at this point that, technically, the law may be broken. Either RS becomes a choice, or it disappears altogether, or it takes part in the social personal compulsory programme. In the sixth form it is an option again. I think that it should be a mixture of all these. As an option it needs to be rejected no more than any other minority subject. What does matter is that the leadership of the school, Headmaster and deputies, are absolutely insistent about its place in the curriculum. But it is for theology to merit its place, and not to depend upon the artificial backing provided by the 1944 Act.

A Head of a Religious Studies Department in a London school wrote this a few years ago, and I think that it sums up the issues very clearly:

> Within my school we have a healthy enough department. We have parity with comparable subjects in allowance, time allocation and to some extent with staffing.
>
> Each year, however, I watch the same process occur. Even with an early interest in the junior forms I see the third years at option time flock to the attractions of other subjects.
>
> For several years this caused me much personal anguish that, despite above average exam success, I had somehow failed as an RE teacher. So I fought for the best position in the option columns until I decided that for the RE teacher there *is* no 'best'.
>
> The real problems of the subject are deeper than any administrative reorganization can solve. The real problems are parents who refuse to allow interested daughters to study a 'useless' subject, careers officers who recommend anything but RE, and the attitude of society which scorns anything connected with 'religion' – so that I must leap around the staff-room brandishing joss sticks to prove I'm not the dull, tweedy caricature of an 'RE teacher', and my A level students suffer near martyrdom rather than divulge that they study the d(r)ead subject.
>
> I think we have a right to expect and demand a definite lead and firm assistance in the alteration of such attitudes – if we really want to survive.

The clause about compulsory 'religious instruction' may have got into the 1944 Act for historical reasons that foreshadowed the comprehensive movement, a movement which was, of course, born out of the 1944 Act. Whether it stays or not, the fact remains that a school is not truly comprehensive unless it offers religious education. Since the spiritual needs of mankind are as much part of his experience as other needs, it follows that the curriculum is deficient without RE. The multi-cultural society requires especially that religious studies is part of every child's upbringing, and there are important educational and cultural reasons for schools to reflect the range of denominations and religions in that society. We are still trying to understand what we mean by this. We have moved from Black Studies for the minority, units on slavery and novels with black characters and Caribbean settings as solutions in themselves. Even searching textbooks for racist comment and bias is peripheral. We are learning to be intellectually much more thorough in all we do; more open to the range of human experience, more aware of our Eurocentric position. For instance, did Columbus 'discover America'? If we are studying a theme, say 'childhood and upbringing', our materials must reflect a genuine multi-cultural experience from the world, a realization of those things which are different, and those things which we have in common.

I suspect that much the same can apply to theological studies. Theology has to rid itself of its Eurocentred language and traditions, and move, in Bishop Trevor Huddleston's words in his Assize Sermon to 'that truly Catholic Universality', which is an 'inter-faith ecumenism – that recognition that dialogue between Hindu and Christian, Muslim and Christian, Buddhist and Christian, must have priority – that should be the aim for us all at this moment in history.' That is why I would want to see theological studies concern itself with more than just Christianity, because I think that understanding comes from seeing something familiar from somebody else's point of view. This is different from comparative religion, and what I think we have done in school is to explore a central religious idea by looking at it from different religious experiences. The focus is the idea and the reason for its importance to mankind. The common themes are the rites of passage; birth, love, suffering, death. (This is described in Jo Gibson's paper.)

The place of RS in the curriculum can also help us to resist those utilitarians now abroad, who are shouting 'back to basics'. They probably include RS, but for the wrong reasons, as a form of moral insurance. It is spanners and bolts versus books; I wish to see literate engineers and practical artists.

The problem here is that the school curriculum is under pressure, and the comprehensive school is similarly pressurized to respond to many of the growing needs of society. All schools are expected to deal with health, drugs, politics, consumer education, or citizens' rights. On and on come the new topics; 'people ought to be educated for this and prepared for that'. It's called the 'exploding curriculum'. At the same time, there is a central debate stemming from the DES about the proportion of compulsory and chosen areas of study. A group of teachers in my school, together with an HMI set out, over two weekends, to take a different look at this question. Instead of saying 'How can we fit each bit into the timetable?', we began with the adolescent children and asked 'What are their needs?'

We came up with a personal curriculum, in which, rather than asking what subject people needed to be taught, we listed all the things which an educated young person should have encountered, and about which he should have thought. This approach to curriculum planning implies that subject areas shall reflect and cover, in their own way, aspects of this *personal curriculum*. For example there is a section recognizing aspects of a person's spiritual needs which we called 'Beliefs and values'. While we presumed that this would be covered only partly by the religious studies department and that other subjects, such as English, history and art would play an essential part, we also presumed that the Religious Studies department would look at other things about which theology had something to say, such as health, friendship, community, partnership, emotion, or society – I can only hint at what I think was a remarkably rich and exciting venture. At this point we are stuck at our school as we consider how this should be applied.

This is what I mean by theology's justifying itself. If it can help us to define what people need and to express it in forms that we can all recognize, then it will have done much to establish itself in the school curriculum. Notice that I have not talked about biblical studies or comparative religion or general religious studies or 'life after school' as I once saw one religious studies syllabus called! If you take as one example the idea that pupils should understand that 'men search for the ideal as well as the real; for immortality as well as mortality', I think that you will see that I have something much more radical and fundamental in mind.

There is a further issue; one which a colleague of mine, George Foster, taught me to see. It is that the school must tackle the need for young adults to join in the public discourse. Since our public conversations are riddled with references, images and metaphors, the frame of cultural reference is as wide as history is deep, and it includes the whole cultural heritage, together with the transmission of its experience and tradition, of which religious studies with its biblical roots is a central part. A child is indeed disabled if he grows up ignorant and unaware of this. Yet, as with other subjects, we have to consider how such an understanding may be achieved, how the cultural richness shall become part of an exploration of the concepts and ideas that people need. Since our public discourse requires and presupposes a knowledge of many traditions and languages, this is part of the rich fabric of public debate, and theological teaching is not alone in facing this task. In the teaching of any subject, we have a duty to widen the awareness of our pupils and theology is one of a number of language systems.

The quality of learning

Perhaps the most important thing is that people should be well taught – imaginatively taught – so that they may want to go on learning. Despite the successes of the comprehensive school, there is still too large a drop out, and it includes people of all abilities. The reasons are complex, but I should like to touch on two aspects of school practice that can disaffect adolescents. One is the way in which secondary schools persist with highly individualized work, when work after school is cooperative. The other is the widespread practice of teachers, which inflicts slow death by comprehension exercises in all subjects. Pages of numbered questions are still the staple stock of commercial publishing houses looking for a living among exhausted teachers desperate for control. The pupils are turned off, and all the fine curriculum development of materials and ideas, like the Schools' Council course *Journeys into Religion*, die dissected in the classroom slaughter-houses.

The way in which secondary schools persist with a highly individual-ized method of study should be compared with the infant school on the one hand, and the university on the other. There is little difference in the quality of learning required by a five-year-old and that required by a sixth former. The infant classroom is a microcosm of education. If we look for a moment at the first years of school when a child is learning to read, much of the activity is similar to what we do at A level. There is good reading with life and character, where there is response to children and their comments. In that situation people listen to what the child has to say, consider his questions and engage in discussion about them. Moreover, as one follows the child's play in the days after the story is told, one can see how the child takes the story and recreates it.

Let me give you an example of how this method may be used in the secondary school. How would you study the Christmas story with children? One lesson which Jo Gibson gave us was to compare the two texts from Luke and Matthew, and ask the pupils to note the similarities and differences. This was as new to me as it was to the pupils when I first did it, and it led to all sorts of questions. Not only was this an act of learning in which we all engaged together, but it was also much richer than the slow death of Christmas by comprehension questions. As a matter of fact this can be done individually as well as in groups, by many different ages and by all levels of ability.

Of course, this method of textual comparison is a practice from the university, and it is biblical study at its best. As the best intellectual practice is suitable for young adolescents, so the finest ideas, like fine wine, have a clarity and perfection which make them the best teaching material. Moreover, children and adolescents would much prefer to work on the 'real thing'. It follows that teachers must be constantly in renewing contact with the university and new ideas. In the case of theology, this is particularly important, so that the artificial distinction with religion may be avoided. As Newman warned us, this distinction breeds 'superstition among the populace and indifference among the intelligent'. An activity in which teacher and learner may engage together does much to avoid this danger at a time when superstition and indifference are as rife as they ever were.

I have deliberately juxtaposed the sixth form, the university and the infant school so as to affirm the over-riding principle of the unity of knowledge, the continuous thread of learning, the seamless web of education. In the infant school, the curriculum should be wide, with drama to act out feelings and situations, art to express ideas (notice how children talk about their pictures as they work, or when they show them to someone else). They must be able to see how things work, to have the opportunity to handle material, make things and operate instruments. They should also be able to make music, to be inventive with many sounds.

So we must not fall into the trap of theology for the sixth form and religious studies for the third form. Although we may call it that, a theological quality must inform and inspire teaching and learning at all levels. There must be a relationship between all stages of education. By that I mean that there must be a similarity in the *method* of teaching at each level age or ability, so that the story of Hecuba may be accessible for all. Hamlet watched the players succeed because the quality of the text that they were given was the best, and because the expectations of the prince were demanding. There was also a serious purpose. We must teach likewise, with quality and expectation. That is why the best writers for children are often the best scholars in the field. Who can better describe the excitement of the findings at Ur of the Chaldees than

Leonard Wooley himself? It is this consistency of a subject and its material that is the real meaning of mixed ability education.

The pastoral setting

I don't think that teaching ever stops within one's subject. I think that we teach within a context. In a city like Birmingham, Liverpool or London, that is particularly the case, and means that a school must be clear about its primary pastoral task. That entails a concern for the care of both staff and pupils, because school, like university, is a community of people and the quality of this pastoral support will affect the academic purpose and success. The concept has its roots deep in theological tradition. So the teaching of any subject, but especially theology, must concern itself with the milieu (see above). The pastoral system of a school should not be separate from the academic – the two should work through each other. Let me expand on that.

When I had responsibility for the welfare and good order of the first three years of my school, I felt that many problems of indiscipline stem from the way we organize our teaching, and the demands that we make on our pupils. Almost any pupil who was sent to me was as the result of confrontation. I particularly remember three boys who had walked out of a lesson, and had gone across to the shops. 'Why?', I asked. 'I felt so depressed. There was so much noise. The teacher wasn't helping me.' 'I was so bored,' said another, 'I didn't understand the work.'

It is incumbent on us, the teachers, to think more about 'our' curriculum and 'their' responses, and to know just how much they can or cannot take. I notice again and again how, when a child falls into trouble, there is nearly always a personal reason for the disorder, a personal dislocation in the child's life which precedes the event at school. When I delve, I find that I get deep into a hopeless family saga. It is a compliment to school that families in distress so often look to it for help, so that I begin to think that the strains and stresses on the modern family are coming to be as great as they were during the last century. The amazing thing is that the children function as well as they do, while I have also come to be far more respectful of the efforts of most families, and wary of the amount of pressure that a school can throw at them.

When we have some very serious incident, we will call all the families of the pupils involved together to sort it out as a group. The level of concern, the expectations of those parents for their children's behaviour, the attitudes they teach, is very high indeed. I meet inadequacy, but seldom lack of concern. In bringing families together, we are seeking to work positively in cooperation, looking for ways of supporting each other. Too often schools take the easy way out and blame the family.

Recently an irate father stormed into my office with his fifteen-year-old son and demanded to know why the boy had not attended school since October, and why we had not told him. I showed him that we had written frequently. As the father turned on the wife, accusing her of not telling him, I realized that he was a man living away from home, who had come to school to assuage his feelings of guilt in abandoning responsibility for his son. I have interviews in which husbands and wives talk to each other only through me, such is their mutual hostility. The numbers of disturbed cases are now so many that the schools' psychological service has difficulty in coping with the referrals we make. We have to have a resident school Education Welfare Officer for our school alone. In Buckinghamshire they have one between ten schools. Our EWO cannot get round all the families. Many children do not know who their father is. Opening a pupil's file is like opening one of Bluebeard's doors. The trouble is that I frequently think that I am opening the seventh door.

Take for instance the case of a boy who was making life a misery for his classmates. I feel somewhat aghast that the children had suffered sexual aggression for two years before it blew up in our faces. On further enquiry it transpired that he was the father of a child at the age of thirteen, while the pregnant mother was seventeen. His father had told him not to marry, but 'to have babies all over the world', that piece of advice is a reflection of his own marriage, which is now falling apart. 'The sins of the fathers shall be visited upon their sons' is psychologically true. Where does my responsibility lie? We have thrown him out, and, in doing that, I am ensuring that he becomes even more exceptionally difficult a teenager, virtually impossible to handle. A girl writing to me from his class said: 'And when it comes to that, there must be something really wrong. He needs help, and I hope you help him to get better.' I was struck by that insight. The mood of the class was that they did not want him back, yet they felt that the priority was the boy's cure.

I tell this story because I think that it epitomizes the issues with which we are faced all the time – the values and beliefs by which we work. In this case, particularly, those values are salvation, forgiveness, help, understanding, the lost individual and the good of the community. The patience and long-suffering of staff and children in my school are truly remarkable. It is difficult not to trade on it. I am sure that you will have noticed that the language of my discussing this case is *theological*, that is a language that helps us to order our experience. In other words, I think that the study of theology cannot be presumed to be something separate from the life we lead. Theology teaches us, above all other disciplines that the *academic* milieu is exposed if it does not work in practice: it is then 'an empty gong or a tinkling cymbal'.

Schools are moral communities, and it is astonishing how much everything we do in school is value loaded. Most of our conversations are about values and expectations. Some of the worst problems in school are caused by our failure to act as we preach, as when staff are unnecessarily vitriolic towards a child, exhibiting a form of verbal abuse which we do not allow among the pupils. Young people spot that kind of contradictions and hate us for it, just as they spot in us neglect, incompetence and laziness.

The subconscious effect of the way in which a teacher treats his pupils is felt particularly acutely in a multi-racial school because of the affinity which may exist with the way in which colonial masters treated slaves. Not far below the surface is their collective unconscious history, and, if staff do not understand that, then they should not teach in a mixed race school. This racial subconscious is of course politically exploited, but it is a psychological factor of which account should be taken. Context is important, and I should like to suggest that, as theological study responds to its milieu and the changing social context of those who do the study, the classroom should seek to relate past to present, while checking it on the anvil of present experience.

Doing theology: a method

It follows that the inner city can be a model both for consideration by theology and for the definition of pastoral care. If the question does not work in Hackney, it probably will not be recognized elsewhere! The city is a crucible for our ideas, an anvil on which to test feelings and insights. As a society we have moved away from the countryside to the metropolis, where we find everything in an acute form; but theology presents a special difficulty – the massive storehouse of pastoral imagery with which it explores itself. The religious metaphors by which we live are drawn more or less entirely from a rural and feudal world, the language from a previous age. However, I think that it presents educational opportunities.

When we take the city as a crucible, we are close to the tradition of St Augustine. His image of *de Civitate Dei* in which to sum up and examine human experience is still an image we use, except that our city is intensely modern and unbeautiful, with the Bull Ring at the centre and the suburbs of Solihull at the outskirts. When we are doing theology, we cannot escape the fact that our images need to be re-examined, and that they have acquired new meaning. T. S. Eliot has shown us how each new work of art becomes a lens through which we view all previous art and experience; in *The Waste Land* he reorganized our feelings about the city, and linked us to Dante's *Inferno*. 'I had not thought death had undone so many', and where the young man curbuncular finds sex without love. Recently, in contrast to Eliot, the film director Tony Garnett has sung his praise to the vitality that is Birmingham's. The city is all this. It is where modern man searches for identity.

If the city is a central image, images and metaphors need continual reinterpretation and reworking. Just as Cereau recast Wagner's *Ring* in the industrial world where the Rhinemaidens guarded a hydro-electric dam, and *Fidelio* was set in a Nazi concentration camp, so the task or process of theology is to pick up continuously shifting resonances of our metaphors and images, ancient and modern. Another reason for this bundle of references is to give a quick sketch of what I have in mind when we are engaged in education. It was L. C. Knights, in the Downside Symposium *Theology and the University*, who pointed out clearly to us that the process of critical teaching and learning is 'making connections'. 'Only connect', as said E. M. Forster. This is what goes on in any good classroom, in all worthwhile English A level work, and I would hope in A level theology as well. The making of connections is a creative activity, and is personal to the group doing it, so that their nature tells us something about the group. The teacher must listen to those connections, just as the theologian has the responsibility to listen for new experience, new meaning. That new meaning can come through created artistic work, whose range includes film, pop lyrics, literature and sculpture. . . There is no division between the reality experienced by man and the way in which he modifies it in an art form. This range of artistic expression in turn modifies the truths and insights of theology.

Finally, I must try to define the kind of theology which I think is likely to emerge in the secular experience, and I can best do that with reference to the personal one. When I talk of things being theological, I mean simply that they have a theological dimension. In other words, we stumble upon the theological through the urban experience, rather than from a body of doctrine. It is an encounter which is more in the form of a quest. I will illustrate this with a personal postscript.

During the Year of the Disabled (1981), a disabled man, interviewed on television, was asked what he would most wish. He replied that he would have liked a wand, which he could wave over all the people of the earth, so as to make them all disabled for six months. He thought that a lot of good would come of that, and that people would understand and *do* something. It is very difficult for any of us to know about something until we experience it. That is why I am often worried about the enclosed language, metaphors and habitual view of the religious position. It might do us all some good to step outside our religious experience for a while, to do without it for a few years, so as to assess what really matters, and to see how much baggage we carry around.

The secret of life is to travel lightly. I often feel that the truly theological person is the one who can jettison baggage, who can live without it, and, for that reason, I am disturbed by the number of false gods and golden calves that exist in our society. People today are captured by concerns and fears. There are parents whose gates are so locked that they cannot reach out to their children, and mothers who are more concerned with how the house looks than with what the child is saying. I was caught out the other day by a friend of mine who was not interested in going with her child to watch a lovely puppet play. How can we expect response and development in our children, if we do not share with them, and enter into their lives? The spirit of childhood should live within us till death; children teach us to listen. The quality of learning in school is no different from that in the family. There are no less deficiencies in educated upper-class families than in urban deprived ones. Personal deprivation is more critical, and by that I mean the way in which we see each other. This is concerned with things like commitment, neighbourliness, concern or toleration, not in theory, but in practice; for example, there is the friend who brings a cooked dish to a family in time of need. But to do that, one has to be on top of life, and so many pressures are on the family that many of us fail to notice others, or to respond.

Coupled with this are the division of generations and the crossing of old social and cultural borders, which are major contemporary experience for many of us today. They are among the most pressing questions raised by adolescents as they embark upon a search in the pluralist and multi-cultural society. These questions are as much on the agenda for 'Theology in the sixth form' as the ultimate questions of life after death, justice or suffering. Moreover, they are also the way round the twin problems of theology in school; namely that it is neither a neutral and cultural study, nor one requiring commitment and faith. It seems to me that commitment and faith are not essential impediments precisely because both are never certain anyway, and are expressed in so many different personal ways throughout our lives.

As a final example, I should like to do a piece of theology on Dover Beach. It is concerned with the 'search in progress'. Many Christians today no longer believe in life after death. I have always been struck by the number of my Christian friends who have held this point of view.

Recently a friend wrote to me, when her husband was dying of cancer. She said, 'he had not that hope, that source of strength (which I really have lately known as never in my life before), I don't mean that crude hope of survival after death either; perhaps more a faith in ultimate purpose and good not wasted'.

It was in reading Buddhist and Hindu literature that I began to understand how man can have a perfectly religious sense of life without dependence upon a literal survival. It seems to me that, in growing through that barrier, we are forced to toughen all our religious sense, because suddenly religious values and propositions must be held for what they are, and not for what they promise. This honesty demands maturity. It also frees a religious sensibility to be *more* and not *less* available to those 'men of good will' who stop short of religious commitment. It immediately catches out those pupils in the third form who thought that they could so easily dismiss their whole year of religious studies. Immediately they are confronted with a reality which they recognize. I believe that as Christianity works together more and more with other faiths, it will grow and develop, and that all world religions will have a more fruitful and less divisive role to play in the world. That is the important thing, that the world should be renewed and become one. That is far-reaching ecumenism.

As I grow older, I am learning that the world is far from normal. I grew up as a boy with such a stable and secure family life that I thought that everyone did just that, and that there were norms by which everyone lived. Now I think that what we call the norms are in fact quite rare, but that there is a grid of civilized normative life and responsible behaviour, which we endeavour to impose on a raw and instinctual humanity, who resist it wildly. Theology knows this as sin and free will and says that mankind is in need of redemption.

Perhaps, in coming to terms with plurality, and in being open to continual change, we do need a theology, not just as an object of study, but also as something that we can use and act out. For that reason I sometimes feel that one of the things missing in my comprehensive school is the sacramental and ritual of Mass. When the day is done, the shouting and anger over, the community needs to come together. It is very difficult to come together successfully in a secular institution. Moreover, when one is dealing with continual cases of misconduct, one needs to act out one's common humanity, and to be able to stand at communion as an equal before God with one's pupils over whom one has charge, 'letting not the sun go down upon one's anger'. Example and acting out are as vital a part of learning as the study.

So perhaps there is a chance that the young man waiting at the bus stop will think about Hecuba on his journey, may even play Hecuba. But what that Hecuba will be like in the future, only God knows, and with our sensitive endeavours, God may be well pleased.

Please accept this paper as the thought of the hurrying man, as he makes his way in 'that sad traffic you call a world'.

NOTES

1. See chapter 9, p. 145, and Introduction.
2. See chapter 8, p. 122.

2   An Experiment at Woodberry Down

Jo Gibson

I must confess that I am a rogue and a renegade – a former Head of Religious Studies who now teaches maths. Because of the nature of my present position, therefore, this paper is a retrospective attempt to describe an experiment at Woodberry Down, which was designed to make religious education relevant in a secular, multi-racial, inner city school, where, according to the national tests that we administer after they have joined us, many of the pupils are of below average ability. For that reason, the aim of the majority of the pupils is a few CSEs, often at grade III or IV. A few pupils attain what we call 'the magic five' – five O levels – each year; but they are definitely part of a minority.

I became involved in RE teaching completely by chance, and not through choice. Although I read theology at university, my own experience of RE in a Grammar School in Birmingham convinced me that I certainly did not want to be a teacher of RE, and immunized me to a great extent against religion. The theology degree completed the immunization process. When I first began to teach, I was employed as an English teacher, but, as it was a time of shortage of specialists, I was enlisted, or told by the Headmaster, that I would be teaching second year RI – Religious Instruction. It was the most unpopular spot in the teaching week, Religious Instruction to a second year group more interested in Arsenal than the Bible; and a further handicap was that I didn't support Arsenal!

My assignment was to teach this class the missionary journeys of St Paul. They had studied the Old Testament prophets in the first year, and they were going to do the life of Jesus in the third year; so, despite my personal antipathy towards St Paul, the greatest misogynist of all time, and my belief that his travels through Asia Minor were rather removed from the life of these children, even though some of them come from Cyprus, Turkey and Greece, that was what I had to teach. On top of this the classes were segregated, because, at that time, Jews, Catholics, Jehovah's Witnesses, Muslims and atheists whose parents had written covering notes for them, did not have to take part. Nevertheless, they weren't withdrawn from the classroom. So, I had to teach a class of whom over a third had been withdrawn from the lesson, and the other two-thirds of whom were not there by choice anyway. Here, I must make my second confession: I didn't try to teach them anything.

The Head of RI at the time was also a Head of House, who had been with the Indian Army. He tended to use his RI lessons for careers guidance, and often recounted his exploits in the Second World War, while, officially, they did a section on African Tribal Religion. A select few opted for O level RE in the fourth and fifth years, and they were taught by the Head of RI in his room, which appeared as an enclave of religion in a secular school, where there were no religious assemblies. Religious assemblies had been abandoned. The staff were antagonistic. The pupils had to sing hymns, and shuffled and talked their way through prayers. No one could control them, and so, in the end, the assemblies were abandoned. I had studied secularization as part of my university course, but at that time it had been a concept. Now it seemed that I was confronted by a truly secular environment. This was reality, and it was I who was suffering from culture shock. Four years spent in teasing out the finer points of ultimate questions does not help in teaching people who are not particularly worried about the questions over which one has agonized oneself. There was no common culture to fall back on. There were no common assumptions. No religious structure bound the school together by its common concern. There was little place for religious questions. Many children's concerns were blatantly materialistic: 'When you're dead, you're dead. Earn as much as you can, buy as much as you can, enjoy yourself as much as you can as soon as possible.'

In the second year of my time at Woodberry Down, RI disappeared from the second year curriculum. It was subsumed into a new integrated studies course, inappropriately entitled 'Man'. It concentrated on geography and history, because many of the teachers in the course steered well clear of anything to do with religion, unless it was far enough removed from everyday life for it to be historical – like gods and goddesses of the Greeks and Romans, the pyramids of Egypt, Ancient Israel. . . For the thirteen hundred pupils of the time, RI was done in one period a week in the third year. There were twenty hours of religious instruction to last a lifetime. Moreover, many staff were antipathetic to this minor incursion of 'indoctrination' in the curriculum of a state school. Couldn't the time be better spent in teaching the children to read?

The Head of RI gradually wound down the department. He didn't buy any new books, he gave away the specialist RI room, and the RI stock cupboard. He continued to teach the Life of Jesus to his three O level candidates in the office. We were left with a record player, a set of records of the New English Bible, and Peake's Commentary on the Bible. If this sounds melodramatic, it can happen, and is happening in some inner city schools. There are schools, including the one with which we are about to amalgamate, where there is no religious education at all. Its place has been usurped by social studies, or – and this is more often the case – that is how the Heads endeavour to comply with the 1944 Act.

So, with my record player and my Peake's Commentary, I became Head of RI. I must admit that the situation that I inherited reminded me very much of Arnold's Dover Beach, where he could hear the long withdrawing roar. But it was out of this secular, materialistic situation that my own teaching, and the syllabus which we used, developed. The third year in many schools which have an optional examination system is the crucial year. It was critical in our school in two respects. It was the only time when all pupils were given RE, and, then, as now, it was the recruiting year for the middle school religious studies option. When I became Head of RE, if that option had declined further, RE would have disappeared from the curriculum completely in the fourth and fifth years, and in the sixth form. I suspect that it would have then disappeared from the third year as well.

That was where our experiment began. The first third year syllabus that we developed to counter this situation was an attempt to relate religion to the life of the pupils without turning it into moral education. It ran counter to the type of religious education advocated in the sixties by Harold Loukes. Loukes saw RE as an investigation in experience, particularly experience in relationships. For him the religious element was implicit. I have never found this a satisfactory model for RE, as it so easily becomes moral or social education, while, further, common ground with other subjects would soon rob this form of religious education of any distinctive nature. For example, the topics covered within the umbrella of interpersonal relationships are dealt with under the umbrella of school English or social studies departments. So one can, in fact, end up with a ridiculous situation where a child who does religious studies, social studies and English is studying the problems of war three times a week in each of those lessons – or the problems of pregnancy, or whatever else is in vogue at that moment.

Our syllabus began with an explanation of what religion is, and an examination of the way in which religion is communicated through myth and symbol. It included the study of two major Christian festivals, Christmas and Easter, since they are the two festivals with a direct relevance to the pupils' own lives. Whether people are Christian or not, in our culture those two festivals impinge on everybody. For example, Muslims living in England have Christmas holidays. On the other hand, a panoramic view of the various religions found in the area round Woodberry Down school was clearly impossible on one period per week. In retrospect, though it was a worthwhile attempt, that first syllabus was totally inadequate. It fell into all the traps that we were trying to avoid, and I believe that it lost its coherence with the children.

The department was composed of non-specialists – a rather disparate group of people. There was the Headmaster, who was an English specialist; there was the deputy Head, who was an historian turned English teacher, and there was a Head of House, who taught music, and, unfortunately was deaf. There was also one other English teacher, who was a committed, rather conservative Christian. Together, we hammered out a syllabus step by step. We learned by failure, and we learned by success which materials worked, which topics we should include for children, and how we should convey understanding. Slowly we formulated the aims and objectives which we wished to achieve. There were four, at which we arrived after three years:

1. To equip pupils with the concepts necessary for an understanding of the areas with which religion concerns itself; and the means, both in language and action, by which religion expresses itself and its particular interpretation (being religiate).

2. To help people to an understanding of and respect for people whose beliefs and customs differ from their own.

3. To encourage pupils to probe and question received traditions, both Christian and non-Christian.[1]

4. To show pupils the contribution, both good and bad, that religion has made to our culture and to other cultures.

As the syllabus continued to develop, it produced its own dynamic, because as we attempted to develop the theological awareness of the children, we also developed our own. I cannot overemphasize the importance of that, since I believe that our syllabus and our teaching must be alive in our minds and imaginations. The crucial factor in the development of this particular syllabus was my own commitment, not to a particular religion, but to the religious search for meaning. In other words, we were concerned with ways of seeing and understanding, and our task was to discover areas and methods of conveying a developing skill.

Our approach and method did not adopt the nineteenth century view of an evolutionary development of religion: animism, polytheism, henotheism, monotheism. That sort of view sees Christianity as the zenith of man's religious achievement; but we tried, at all costs, to avoid the view that 'the heathen in his blindness bows down to wood and stone'. Anyone with a knowledge and sympathy with Hindu religious practice would recognize the fallacy and over-simplification of that particular statement. It is, nevertheless, a trap into which many RE teachers can fall, and, of course, it is a criticism that can easily be transferred to certain branches of Christianity. Nor were we concerned with comparative religion in the sense that it was a new obsession of the liberal mind. There one was supposed to set out in parallel columns the beliefs and customs of all known religions, contemporary with or antecedent to Christianity, to note their similarities, and to account for them all by labelling them products of the human mind.

We were trying to avoid the Cook's tour, supermarket shelf approach. 'Here are five religions, choose the one that suits you best.' We were not providing a faith to live by, and we did not accept the Troeltschian view that Christianity transcends other religions. We did not treat other religions as if they were transcended by Christianity, a view which I, personally, find abhorrent, but which still persists in RE teaching, and is a consequence of the all-inclusive, yet exclusive dichotomy within Christianity itself. Johnston, writing in a book on comparative religion in education in 1970 puts that particular and worrying view. 'Christianity,' he says, 'is the religion to end all religions. It implies a judgement upon all other religious systems ancient and modern. Truth, finality and clarity are given in Christ.'[2] In a multi-racial situation, such a view seems both inappropriate and rather presumptuous. It is both intellectually and theologically dishonest. So, what were we doing?

If there is to be a label, it is that we were doing a 'phenomenological study', but, even that description I find inadequate, because we were trying to elicit an imaginative reaction from pupils to the materials that we presented. We sought for empathy and understanding, even if they wished to refute the claims of a particular religious interpretation. As teachers we were initiators, awakeners and enablers. We were not initiating people into a particular branch of religion, however, but to the quest for meaning. We were awakeners to certain issues that might easily have been avoided. We could almost be called 'confronters', or enablers in terms of providing critical skills and concepts which would enable children to explore more fully and express more deeply their own thoughts and feelings, and to clarify their own experience.

For example, the core of the third year course was the search for order and meaning by different religious groups. The themes were myth, symbol, ritual and festival. The anchor points of the syllabus were crucial stages in human life and experience, like birth, puberty, marriage and death.[3] Because we were not teaching from a confessional viewpoint we were not providing definitive answers to questions raised, but were rather exploring as much as the children whom we were teaching. That is why teaching about rites of passage has an important place in the syllabus which we developed. By basing our teaching on aspects of experience common to all mankind, we tried to help pupils to understand how religion is concerned with questions as old as humanity itself. We hoped that a deeper knowledge and understanding of the way in which man has tried to interpret his experience of life, and of the expression of that interpretation in the rites of passage, would help pupils in their own search, both in terms of seeking the meaning of life, and in attempting to bring order to their experience of it.

This change in direction produced important results. For the first time in my experience of the school, the rest of the staff began to agree that religious studies had an important role in the curriculum. There was an increased willingness for them actually to involve themselves in the teaching. Secondly, there was an acceptance of the subject by the children and their parents, and there was no further withdrawal from religious studies or religious education. Everyone was expected to study RS in the third year, in the same way as they studied geography or history. Thirdly, there was a new openness to the subject on the part of the children, a new interest in religion. The attitude of 'I'm not religious, why do I have to do this?' disappeared (I hope).

Through our approach, it also became possible for us to study Christianity in the classroom without great groans and protests, while there was also some decline in the prejudice of pupils against other religious and racial groups, though the lack of maturity and under-standing was still more pronounced in the middle school than the third year. There was an expansion of the department in that, instead of three or four pupils taking religious studies in the fourth and fifth years, the group jumped to 15–20 pupils. There was also an increasing take up of religious studies in the sixth form. One worrying aspect, however, was that, even though some children would have liked to have continued with their religious studies, the pressure on them not to do so was still great. Many parents do see religious studies as a luxury, something for people who want to become priests and nuns. For that reason, when we were teaching the syllabus, the material was very important to success. It was essential to use as many aids as possible, such as video, drama, slides and textual material. We were also using booklets which we produced ourselves, rather than textbooks. At the same time, we were trying to use the experience of the children themselves, particularly in the neighbourhood of the school. But that is probably the most difficult thing.

In the middle school – the fourth and fifth years – the change from CSE and O level syllabuses based on the study of the Gospels, to a wider examination of humanity's religious quest was natural as a consequence of what was happening in the third year. The work of the third year, where we were looking at the responses of the different religions to the quest for order, patterns and meaning, was continued into the fourth and fifth years. The main difference in the middle school was that, since we were given more time, we were able to look in greater depth at the religions involved, and to encounter more aspects of different systems of belief. We followed Smart and his list: mythology, ritual, history, ethic, doctrine, the experience of being a member.

The importance of this phenomenological study of religion, described by Ninian Smart, is that it can both take seriously the experience on which man's religious awareness is based, and, at the same time, avoid giving the inference that one religious tradition is likely to have a claim to truth prior to any other. This can be specifically grounded in Smart's list. For example, in the introduction to *The Phenomenon of Religion* Ninian Smart writes:

> . . .first the phenomenology of religion illuminates the necessity for the rather heavy contextualisation of religious utterances. For instance, some attention is paid here to the notion of the Focus of a rite (such as Christ in the case of the Eucharist). From this it is apparent that the existence or otherwise of Christ has to be treated experientially in the context of ritual (e.g. worship). Similarly, of course with God the Father and the God of the Muslims and so forth. This makes the task of analysing the existence claims quite a subtle one, bound to elude a straight verificationist model. Second. . . a theory of myth bears a similar message, except that. . . a proper treatment of myth involves the assumption of the numinosity of the divinities (or of some of them) appearing in the stories, which are themselves coordinated to ritual activities.[4]

Ninian Smart continues by saying that this means that an important question for the philosophy of religion is the nature and 'validity' of the experience of the Holy (in which he admits his indebtedness to Rudolph

Otto). For the teacher this last point gains more practical expression in an article by John Marvell.

> If the phenomenological approach is to be adopted for religious education, three points should be borne in mind. First the teacher will be concerned with man's religious experience and that this is distinctive from any other form of experience. . . Secondly there is the need to develop new teaching materials. . . Lastly teachers of religious education should be equipped. . . both in-service and initial courses, in the future, should equip the teacher to understand and be able to communicate to others that which is universal in religion and that which is particular to various times and places.[5]

In our case the study was limited to the five religions that could be found in the neighbourhood of the school: Christianity, Judaism, Islam, Sikhism, Hinduism. We particularly concentrated on Judaism, because the school was situated in a strongly orthodox Jewish area, with a large body of Hasidic Jews. The aims and objectives remained the same, and there were moments of success, as when a child would say, 'I couldn't understand them before, but now I can see why they're like they are.' Success also meant the realization that religion is an integral part of life for many people. It's not something divorced from life – an appendage or superstition. It's not a pre-scientific stage, it's not a pre-technological state, it's not an aberration, and it's not an irrational escape from reality. At CSE we had to use Mode III as there was no appropriate syllabus available in Mode I.

The concern of this symposium is with theology at 16+. This paper has concentrated on work which we did with younger pupils. However, to me the relationship is quite clear. The foundations of theological exploration must be laid further down the school. I would agree with Simon Clements[6] that thirteen seems to be an appropriate age at which to begin laying these foundations. The rest is just a continuation. The method employed in sixth form teaching – here I am talking about a non-academic sixth form – is no different from the method employed in teaching those third formers. The aims are no different. The one constraint on the sixth form and the middle school, however, is the examination system, and, in particular, the content of existing examinations in RE. Too many examinations still seem to concentrate on factual knowledge, or they have a section on the application of Christian principles to the great problems of the century. Many of our pupils who do not have a Christian allegiance find it very difficult to engage themselves with this.

I have tried to propose something else, and to show how it worked in the secular school.

APPENDIX

The third year syllabus of the Religious Studies Department at Woodberry Down is a particularly good example of the way in which Jo Gibson's attitude to Religious Education worked in practice. The 1978 course was organized into interrelated units, so that it was possible to return to themes which had been examined earlier, and build on them during the year, rather than to treat them as isolated topics. This facilitated the reinforcement of major concepts, since they could be considered from different points of view as the course progressed. The aims of the syllabus were:

(i) To equip pupils with the concepts necessary for an understanding of the areas with which religion concerns itself, and the means, both in language and action, by which religion expresses itself and its particular interpretation of the world.

(ii) To help people towards an understanding of, and respect for people whose beliefs and customs differ from their own.

(iii) To encourage pupils to probe and to question received traditions, both Christian and non-Christian.

(iv) To show pupils the contribution that religion has made to our culture.

There were ten units in the syllabus, and a particularly important aspect of it was the way in which it showed how religion marks man's attempt to make sense of his experience of life and the world around him.

The units were as follows:

1. Patterns and cycles

This aimed to show how human beings react to the world around them by asking questions and looking for ways to order their experience. Illustration was provided by a study of early religion, and of the way in which it may be seen as representing man's attempt to understand his experience of the world. In particular the syllabus concentrated on four areas:

(i) *the search for meaning and order*: this was concerned with the way in which the life cycle, together with the solar and lunar cycles, may be connected with religious festivals in the course of the year. This is particularly important for those who live in large cities, and who do not have first-hand experience of the agricultural year.

(ii) *questions about fact and questions about meaning*: (e.g. myths, legends and religious language).

(iii) *the connection between the natural cycle and religion*: e.g. the Christianization of Christmas, the seasons, the Golden Bough).

(iv) *human beings' attempt to control the external world*: (festivals at mid-summer and mid-winter; fertility rites; dramatic re-enactment).

2. Initiation

This emphasized the way in which religions usually have ceremonies to mark the important stages in the life cycle of the individual. In other words, at this stage the life cycle is examined, just as the cycle of the seasons was examined in the first unit. In view of its obvious pertinence to the pupils, the unit concentrated on puberty.

(i) *the importance of puberty and becoming an adult*: this included an assessment of what makes an adult, and of the nature of individual responsibility.
(ii) *rites of passage*: the tests for adulthood*.
(iii) *initiation into the religious community*: this included the Hindu Sacred Thread Ceremony, the Jewish Bar Mitzvah/Bat Mitzvah and Christian Confirmation.

*The importance of rites of passage is connected with the way in which man's life-experience marks the starting point for his religious understanding.

3. Self

This unit links with the questions posed in 2(i) on the importance of puberty and becoming an adult. In particular the unit aims to pose the following questions:

Who has made me what I am?
Who am I?
What do I want to become?
How much control do I have?
How much choice do I have over what I become?

In so far as these are 'ultimate questions' they point to the way in which religion may be seen as a search for understanding and meaning rather than as a simple proclamation of truth.

4. Myth

This unit links with the first one on patterns and cycles. It examines the way in which human beings use stories to answer the questions which they pose about themselves and the world. This points to the need for people to have a religious vocabulary, and focusses pupils' attention on issues which might otherwise have been avoided. It also enables them to know what religious words actually mean. In Christianity an example of this is the way in which Spirit=breath=wind, and so has the implication of a life force. The unit may also be linked to units 6 & 7 on festivals, since myth is often an integral part of festival. The units may be subdivided into:

(i) *creation myths*
(ii) *myths about the origin of sin and death*

(iii) *myths about life after death*
(iv) *modern myths about the struggle between good and evil*

A particularly important part of this unit is concerned with the introduction of the concept that truth is not always empirical, and that myths are not always necessarily intended as alternatives to a scientific interpretation of the world. This leads to consideration of the relationship between fact and meaning, and of the way in which the good historian is concerned with the causes of events as well as with the dates on which things happen.

It is useful to refer back to the types of question asked by human beings and the forms of answer which are suitable to different types of question.

5. Symbols

This unit is concerned with the use of symbols and their importance in both secular and religious life. Examples are:

Mathematical symbols
Punctuation
Map signs
Road transport signs
The Jewish skull cap
Light, water, ritual (e.g. the Sikh Silver Thread)

This unit is of great importance, since reference to symbol should be made in the units on initiation, festival and myth.

6. Midwinter festivals

Festival will have been mentioned in connection with the first unit on cycles. This unit concentrates on festival in greater detail, and it should include revision of the idea of the natural cycle. In particular it is important that three areas should be covered:

(i) *pagan midwinter*: including saturnalia and its continuing influence.
(ii) *Christmas*: including a study of Luke/Matthew and the nativity in art.
(iii) *Channukah*: the Jewish festival of light.

This unit demonstrates the way in which the cycles of the seasons have been connected with the growth of man's religious observance in a number of different traditions.

7. Spring festivals

The crucial idea in this unit is concerned with the way in which rebirth and resurrection are seen as being represented by the natural cycle. Three festivals were covered in this unit:

(i) *Hindu Holi*
(ii) *Jewish Passover*
(iii) *Christian Easter* (including reference to pagan elements)

The section on Passover should examine its importance in the history of the Jews, and the ideas of slavery and freedom. This is very important in

Hackney, where the exodus from a homeland will have been the experience of the parents and grandparents of many of the pupils. Slavery will also have been part of the folklore or inherited tradition of people whom they have met in their families.

In studying the Passover, pupils will be helped if they see that the prescription for eating the passover meal in Exodus 12 is a type of liturgical rubric.

The difficulties and contradictions in Christian texts should not be avoided (see Simon Clements in ch 1, p. 25) on the nativity stories.

Note: a similar comparison was also done on the resurrection stories.

    Texts: The Resurrection of Jesus in Matthew and Luke.
             Exodus 12 in the New English Bible.
             The Seder Meal.

8. Marriage

Marriage is the third major stage in a person's life celebrated by all religions. In conjunction with birth, it is one stage which will involve the majority of pupils within the next ten years. Reference should be made to cycles and symbols.

The use of films and slides of weddings of different traditions is desirable.

9. Death

This is the concluding unit for the study of cycles, and it is concerned with the place in religion of the last of the stages in the life of the individual. It should refer back to myth and symbol, and include consideration of different beliefs about life after death or lack of it.

10. Religion in Britain today

This unit could be either the starting point for the course, or its conclusion. In so far as very few pupils will continue to study religion in the middle school, it is essential that they should have some knowledge of the religious communities in Hackney and East London. An important section within this unit covers the basic features of Judaism, including information about the Hasidim.

Material available to teachers

One of the chief difficulties for a Head of Department who wishes to introduce a syllabus of this kind is that teachers must be helped to gain access to the relevant information. Two examples are given of the types of material used at Woodberry Down. In the first, information is given about puberty rites, and the way in which they are related to initiation ceremonies. This is relevant both to the relationship of religion to the cycle of a person's life and to its connection with rites of passage. The questions which arise are intended to stimulate class discussion and to focus the attention of pupils on issues which might otherwise have been left out of consideration.

The section on Hallowe'en is intended to demonstrate the way in which religion may take over popular practice and use it in a new way. It also demonstrates some of the differences in outlook between city dwellers and countrymen. This distinction is important if religious education is to be properly understood in a secular and urban society. It is also important for the teacher to select the right audio-visual material. In particular good material on weddings and funerals in different traditions is available.

The examples given are intended to show something of the way in which a Head of Department may help other teachers, in particular when they are non-specialists. Nevertheless suggestions about a plethora of material, which may cease to be available, have been avoided.

1. *Puberty rites and initiation ceremonies (rites of passage)*

(*a*) *Hindu* The sacred thread ceremony

The ceremony takes place in the boy's home. His religious teacher – guru – performs the ceremony with the boy's father. They read or sing parts from the Hindu scriptures. Then a cord with three threads is placed across the boy's shoulders. The thread is worn for the rest of the boy's life. It marks a new beginning, and the boy is known as 'twice-born'. He has to begin studying the Hindu sacred writing: he promises to study hard, to avoid luxury and to dedicate himself to his god. There is no ceremony for girls.

(*b*) *Jewish* Bar Mitzvah/Bat Mitzvah (Son/Daughter of the Law)

This service, too, is primarily designed for boys, although there is an equivalent for girls. It marks the time when the boy assumes full adult religious responsibility. First he has to have special lessons from the Rabbi (Jewish teacher). He has to learn how to read Hebrew, and to study the Torah (the laws of behaviour contained in the OT). He then sits a special exam.

The special service takes place on the Sabbath (Saturday) nearest to his thirteenth birthday. For the first time he is allowed to read from the scroll of the Torah in the synagogue. When he has finished reading – in Hebrew – the Rabbi reminds him of his responsibilities to obey the Torah. He is now held totally responsible for his behaviour, and is regarded as equal with the other men in the synagogue.

The boy says a special prayer: 'Today I enter the community, as one worthy to be numbered to form a congregation for public worship and to assume the full responsibilities of a Jew. Help me O merciful Father. . .' There is usually a big party afterwards to celebrate the event.

(c) *Christian* Confirmation

In Christianity babies are usually baptized or Christened (except in Baptist and allied churches). At the ceremony Godparents make vows to help the child to grow up as a Christian. Then, when the child has grown up, to the age of about fourteen (compare the practice of the Catholic Church), he/ she makes vows for himself.

Confirmation usually follows a course of instruction in Christian beliefs. The ceremony is often performed in church by a bishop, but in the Free Churches this is done by a minister. The bishop asks three questions: Do you turn to Christ? Do you repent of your sins? Do you renounce evil? If the person says 'yes' to all three questions the bishop lays his hand on his or her head and says: 'Confirm O lord this your servant with your Holy Spirit.' From then on the person is responsible for his own behaviour. He can now receive the holy communion.

These three ceremonies take place at about the same age – 13/14. (Two exceptions are 'baptism' in the Baptist/Pentecostalist Churches, which takes place after 'conversion' – and confirmation in the Catholic Church, which usually takes place at seven).

Questions arising:

1. Is thirteen a good age to assume responsibilities? Why thirteen?
2. In what way does society show that a young person is ready to assume adult responsibilities? What does being an adult entail? (e.g. changing attitude to parents, pubs, X films/AA category, the vote).
3. Has anyone in the group been involved in one of these ceremonies, or something similar?
   What. . .? Why. . .? How. . .? Has it made a difference?
4. In some societies young people are tested. For instance, Aborigines have to prove that they can survive in the wilderness before they can become adults. Are there any tests like this in our society?
5. Why do so many societies have a special ceremony to show that a young person has become an adult?

2. *Hallowe'en*

In the dark years before Christianity came to Britain, there were two seasons on the earth. There was the season of sowing, which was the season of light and life. There was the season of saving, when nothing grew, and the earth died. This was the season of darkness, when the days were short, nights were long, the weather was bitter, and the forces of darkness ruled.

The Druids, the priests of the old religion, remembered these two seasons in their holy days. In May they held the festival of Beltane. In October they held the festival of Samain. At Samain they lit fires to guard them from the evil forces which were all around them. They burnt people in wicker cages. The fires were an appeal to the sun, as well as a protection against the demons.

The festival of Samain was held at the end of October, and it was a great festival of the dead. On the night of Samain, which we now call Hallowe'en, goblins ran screaming through the land. The souls of those who had died during the year were dragged from the bodies of birds and animals, where they had taken refuge, and taken to the land of the dead underneath the earth. Samain was the night when the forces of darkness ruled. Clustered around the bonfire, each person in the village placed a stone to form a circle round the bonfire. In the morning, if their stone had fallen over, it meant that they would die in the coming year.

Then came Christianity. The old religion survived, so the Christian priests tried to make the practices of the old religion part of the new one. Instead of making an offering of a human being to guard against demons, they persuaded people to sacrifice an ox to the saints of the Catholic Church. November 1st became *All Saints Day*. (All Hallows Day in Old English). October 31st became *All Hallows Even*, the original form of the word Hallowe'en. But the old beliefs persisted. Bonfires were lit, and people prepared charms to protect themselves against demons. They put out small offerings of food for the dead. Some people rejected the new religion completely; they became 'witches'. They worshipped the old gods still. People believed that witches had special powers at Hallowe'en. They could change into animals, or they could fly across the sky on sticks. They sacrificed and drank blood. They consorted with Satan.

Hallowe'en remained the night on which people stayed indoors. If one left one's house, one might be snatched by a goblin or witch, and one's soul would be dragged to hell.

It was in the nineteenth century that Hallowe'en began to lose its importance. Many people left the countryside and went to live in towns, and cities. They no longer feared demons and goblins. They forgot the old customs which no longer made sense to them, because they did not have to grow crops, or worry about harvest, or live in a cottage in the middle of nowhere.

Here are some old Hallowe'en customs:

(*a*) Place an apple beneath your pillow. You will dream of a future lover.

(*b*) Eat the flesh of an apple. Cast the skin over your left shoulder. The skin will fall into the shape of your true lover's initial.

(*c*) Cut an apple into eight pieces. Eat seven pieces sitting in front of a mirror. Hold the eighth piece on a knife. You will see your future husband's reflection in the mirror.

NOTES

1. See chapter 8, p. 125.
2. W. Johnston, *The Still Point*, New York 1970.
3. See chapter 8, p. 126.
4. Ninian Smart, *The Phenomenon of Religion*, Macmillan 1973.
5. John Marvell, 'Phenomenology and the Future of Religious Education', *Learning for Living*, vol 16, no 1, Autumn 1976.
6. See chapter 1, p. 26.

3   The Place of Theology in a Confessional School

Peter Hastings and Geoffrey Turner

Historically, confessional schools were created as safe havens from a pagan secular world where the children of 'the faithful' could worship, be instructed and initiated into the sacraments along with their traditional school education. Whether this was ever a realistic or desirable project is doubtful, but it is now so unrealistic as to be pure fantasy and it is certainly not desirable that we perpetuate the fantasy of the confessional school, specifically the Catholic school, as 'a community of faith'. The school as 'community of faith' presupposes that virtually all the members of this community, staff and pupils, in some sense 'have the faith'. But not all Catholic schools even have a majority of committed Christians among their staff and there are fewer schools that have a majority of Christian pupils.[1] With falling rolls we increasingly find Catholic schools accepting a significant proportion of non-Catholic pupils – we know of one with a 50% non-Catholic intake – and the intake of Church of England schools has always been very mixed. The proportion of non-Catholics in our school is around 15–20%, though some of these are Christians.

The degree of commitment of those who call themselves Christian is also very variable. To call a pupil a Christian is not necessarily to do more than give him a cultural label. He/she may indeed be a committed, practising, conscientious Christian. But he may not have been in a church since baptism, or he may be taken unwillingly to church, or he may be sent by parents who never go, or he may want to distance himself a bit from the religion of his upbringing while he goes in for some serious self-questioning in early adulthood. Whatever the case, in terms of religious commitment it is a very mixed bunch that we find in the classroom of a confessional school. It is very difficult to estimate in practice as church attendance is a poor guide, but we may guess that around a third of the pupils would want to affirm their Christian identity.

Nonetheless, in a confessional school most of its members may be assumed to be part of an identifiable cultural-religious tradition which is Christian, or we may assume that in coming to such a school most of its members will respect that tradition and may be prepared to investigate the meaning and practice it represents. In the context of a confessional school an earnest search for truth can be fostered within an inherited Christian tradition. Most adolescents and young adults have a natural desire to question things and look for truth, yet we do them no service if we trick them into imagining that the truth about reality comes predetermined and instantly available like plastic wrapped cheese in Sainsbury's. *We* may believe that some fragment of the transcendent reality of God can be grasped in the Christian tradition, but they have to discover it and it must be fought for.

It is not the purpose of the confessional school, we would all agree, to indoctrinate children. But if we really believe that, we must also respect the liberty of the children in our schools and not *compel* them against their conscientious wishes to worship or confess orthodox beliefs. Such compulsion would be not only immoral but counterproductive; it only causes resentments and is educationally and religiously harmful. An earlier Downside Symposium on Religious Education (1968) referred to a survey which showed that where there is a high level of apparent religious adherence by pupils in the public performance of their school, *there* was the lowest actual adherence. It would seem that the most successful Christian schools are those which encourage a thoughtful consideration of religious commitment but do not rely on a conspicuous public show of it. We have no compulsory worship in our school and believe that voluntary worship and free discussion in an open search for truth must be the basis of all education.

The purpose of the confessional school, then, is not to protect or indoctrinate, but to search for truth, to raise questions, and to enter into conversations which are going on in society and the church. The raising of questions comes naturally to young people in any sphere, and in the confessional school this can take place within the stability of a given cultural context and can be guided and helped by knowledgeable and sympathetic teachers. Furthermore, our teaching must promote an active criticism of the practice of society, including the society of the church. There is, of course, a pluralism of belief and practice in society and the Christian church and it would be dishonest to pretend that we live in a monolithic society or church which is not subject to historical change. We must introduce our pupils to these facts of life while we can still help them make sense of it rather than allow them to become cynical and dismissive after they have left school, when they will discover that reality does not correspond to some pious fiction. If a French cardinal dies of a heart attack in the arms of a prostitute, if popes have murdered, if some bishops have supported oppressors and torturers of the poor, if the church has changed its mind on a variety of issues, our pupils had better find out about it rather than be given an artificially rosy picture of the church. We should resist the long standing tendency of confessional schools to picture a lily-white uncorrupt church as though our commitment were to the institution rather than to Christ.

If the general aim of the confessional school is to search for truth and love, theology aims to do just this in a narrower religious sphere, specifically in the Christian tradition. By the time our pupils reach adolescence, say from the age of fourteen, they must be encouraged to inspect the Christian luggage they have been obliged to carry through childhood. Theology aims to develop an understanding of personal religious experience; affirmation comes later and is an adult act. One of our major problems in a confessional secondary school is dealing with children whose experience of Christianity has been dominated by the pressure they have been put under by their family, priest or primary school to affirm allegiance when preparing for first communion, confession and confirmation, while having precious little understanding of what they have been asked to affirm. Those who have not been carrying any ecclesiastical luggage may be introduced to Christianity for the first time and we encourage them to develop a sensitivity for and do some serious thinking about questions of religious meaning and personal commitment.

It would be presumptuous to presuppose belief and commitment among our pupils, but we may expect them to engage in some hard thinking about these issues. Theology is a human not a divine activity, and it involves people who think. It is judgmental. Pupils in a secondary school have to be helped to form personal judgments about their own position with regard to the claims to truth and the social practice of the Christian church in the light of their personal experience.

It is a pretty mature task that we are setting our pupils, but experience has shown us that it is well within their grasp. Before adolescence judgmental thinking on such a scale is not possible and should not be attempted, but theology can be done and should be done in the sixth form and perhaps, the three years preceding the sixth form. Our experience is that it is a good thing for pupils to have a year left fallow after their primary school religious education and to begin a more adult form of theology in Year 3 (13–14 years). As pupils become intellectually and emotionally more mature, the more penetrating their theological thinking can be. Some pupils, sometimes the religious ones, prefer to avoid a personal scrutiny of their beliefs or behaviour, and while we cannot expect them to share our way of seeing things we can expect them to be involved in this questioning. Many others are only too fascinated by participating in an investigation of religious belief and discovering just what the Christian gospel entails. Whatever the difficulties in practice, Christian theology must be attempted, for what is the purpose of sinking millions of pounds into confessional schools if a space is not created in them for theological investigation and discovery?

Theology in secondary schools need not be excessively academic. The academic level at which it operates must be that which is most suitable to enable self-discovery by the children involved. Different pupils have different needs, different starting-points and different intellectual abilities. The problem is to cater for these many personal requirements, and after a general introductory year we have instituted a series of termly options so that each pupil can choose what is most suitable. This allows sufficient opportunity for pupils to follow their own interests into areas of theology which matter to them. If pupils want to raise questions about the eucharist, or examine beliefs about life after death, or investigate the differences between Christianity and Buddhism, then we must allow them the time and resources to do so even in these hard pressed times, and we must help them to find the language to talk about these things. Too often confessional schools have perpetuated a naive, child-like version of Christianity. Too often they have limited themselves to passing on information about Christianity, frequently about matters irrelevant to the children. Who among our generation has not suffered a term's work on Paul's missionary journey's? Would we now inflict it, or its equivalent, on our pupils? No. We must provide a space in which decent theological work can be done, but let *them* make the running and we will provide the educational tools that they need.

Producing fixed, detailed, nationally agreed syllabuses is not much help, indeed they can stifle open enquiry. What is important is not so much what pupils learn as how they use what they learn. What a school needs is graduate theology teachers with a wealth of resources who can follow the course of a discussion where the children take it, or who can guide it on to fruitful new paths. Amateur teachers, no matter how well intentioned, are not likely to be able to cope with the spontaneity of theology teaching, and we have always maintained an all-graduate department. At present this consists of four teachers.

Within this freedom to explore interests, we insist that all our pupils look at some topics which are central to the Christian tradition: the God-question, for example, and the significance of Jesus of Nazareth. No pupil should pass through a Christian confessional school without having discovered something of the Christian message about God or without being invited to consider what he believes about Jesus.

The importance of teaching theology well has little to do with passing examinations and most of our work at The Trinity School is non-examination work; theology for its own sake, we might say. It is, however, important that some respectable academic theology is done in the sixth form of a confessional school. At all levels the demands that theology makes on its students must be comparable with other subjects, and its teachers must equal or better the competence of other teachers. In the sixth form this means that *any* self-respecting confessional school will be pursuing an A level course in theology or religious studies. The scholarly pursuit of theology in the sixth form can act as a focus for the non-examination work done elsewhere in the school, and, reciprocally, A level courses will only get recruits if theology is done in a stimulating and helpful way lower down the school. We have a need for sound and exciting syllabuses and we believe we have just such a syllabus at The Trinity School. It is a tough syllabus but a number of our students regularly go on to read theology or philosophy for their degrees.

This examination course and the kind of theology outlined here could be done avantageously in all types of school – with some modification of content for each school with its different pupil intake and its different needs – but where can we expect decent Christian theology to be done if it is not being done in confessional schools?

Examination results, however, are a secondary matter. It is the aim of this confessional school, at least, to produce mature thinking young adults who have discovered a commitment to Christ or who have a respect for what Christianity represents, based on a sound critical understanding of the Christian tradition, and who behave in a way that indicates a concern for truth and love whether they believe this is to be found in God or not.

A note by Mervyn Davies, formerly Head of Theology, and currently Principal of St Brenda's VI Form College, Keynsham, Bristol, on the practical aspects of teaching The Trinity School Mode 2 Advanced Level Syllabus in Religious Studies

It is commonly forgotten by many people in the church, who should know better, that theology, like education, is both a study and a pursuit.

It is not a subject which expects a student to be passive, to develop only the powers of factual recall, for it is essential to good theology that the student should develop the capacity for understanding, or for judgment based on evidence, so that he may articulate his own views from the basis of what he has studied. It should be the subject in which the teacher and those being taught stand side by side in a common endeavour, rather than one in which a corpus of knowledge is transferred from one person to another.

In this respect, theology is essentially different from catechesis. The latter is a process in which one person learns to accept the intellectual or moral position of another, whereas theology is more open-ended – a search for the truth about God and the mystery of existence, so that, in many ways, the questions become more important than the answers. Indeed, one of the most important tasks of successful teaching of theology, in my view, is that it should help students not only to understand, but also to feel at ease with the process of theological questioning. In this respect, teachers of RE make their own task difficult, when they confuse catechesis with RE, and represent religion as having too many answers, since this only serves to reinforce the view that it has no answers at all!

The Mode 2 Advanced Level Syllabus in Religious Studies produced by The Trinity School in Leamington Spa has been in use for twelve years now. It is based on the assumption that theology is a lively activity, where there should be a dialogue and sometimes a clash of minds as well! It is an attempt to get away from a passive approach to theology, and, for that reason, the syllabus tries to help students to discover what theology really is. It follows that the learning methods by which students find out how to become 'theologically active' are crucial. The acquisition and development of skills – many of which overlap with those needed in other subjects, such as English and the sciences – are primary, and among these are the ability to engage in discussion, to reflect upon experience, to research with others and independently, and to put forward a well-argued point of view. These things are not acquired if the teaching is predominantly didactic or teacher centred. Indeed it is important that the student should learn that his teacher is one resource among others, which include books, his colleagues, and, not least, himself.

In fact, one often finds that the hidden message contained in a lot of teaching is that the learner himself has little to offer – a view similar to the church's attitude to the laity before Vatican II! For that reason it is important that a student's own vocabulary should be developed so that he can understand what he hears and reads. Yet if this is really to be of use, he must be helped to gain the confidence that what he has to say will be heard and valued, and this is in accord with current opinion, which recognizes that healthy feelings of self-worth are essential to successful learning and the realization of potential. Thus, the Mode 2 course requires teachers who are not only theologically literate themselves, but also open minded to students, and, like St Anselm, *quaerens intellectum*. They must be skilled in leading discussion, in giving tutorials and in supervising worthwhile research. If this appears to be a tall order, it is, perhaps, because we need to change our ideas about what real teaching is, and, therefore, the way in which we train teachers, so that this may be the norm for good ones.

These are the reasons why this syllabus has always been taught with a 'mixed economy' of methods. A central feature has always been the weekly seminar, in which every member of the theology staff and every student contributes one paper based on his own research in each term, and to which outside speakers are invited from time to time. Since a great deal of emphasis is placed on resources, the provision of an adequate library was a top priority. It includes many volumes which an undergraduate might be expected to consult.

Successful sixth form teaching often depends on good preparatory work lower down. There is good evidence now which supports the view that there is too great a gulf between the approach to learning in years 1–5 and that which pertains in the sixth form. Suddenly the student is expected to be able to discuss, to use the library extensively, to work independently and to construct hypotheses based on experience or research.[2] Many students flounder at the apparent enormousness of this task, so that it is clear that these skills must be taught progressively throughout the secondary school, and earlier, if real maturity is to be attained in the sixth form.

In the theological arena, however, there are other hurdles. The main obstacle to theological understanding and religious growth is fundamentalism, which has two main forms. First there is a fundamentalism concerned with authority, which assumes that there is no real place for conscience and the individual's informed judgment. Secondly there is a fundamentalism concerned with scripture, which assumes that there is only one kind of way in which anything can be true. The A level syllabus is very much concerned to discuss this problem. Nevertheless, it must also be tackled with discussion and investigatory work by the third year of secondary school. By then, as Goldman and others have shown, pupils are better able to understand the many facets of such concepts as 'truth' and 'right'.

Learning, however, is not linear but cyclic, and the kind of learning encouraged by this syllabus is designed to bring such understanding to maturity, and to give young people at least a glimpse of how enthralling theology can be. This is done both by breaking new ground, and by looking again at other problems in a different and deeper way.

APPENDIX

The Trinity School Mode 2 Advanced Level Syllabus in Religious Studies

Aim

To explore traditions of religious and theological understanding in depth and to think critically and constructively about human existence with the aid of a scholarly study of religious writings. To understand these texts against a wider background of theological and secular thought in various historical periods. To lead the student from an initial appropriation of critical method, through an understanding of a variety of texts and associated problems, to a personal engagement with a modern author who reflects the interests and concerns of the student in the contemporary climate.

Objectives

Candidates should be able to:
1. Show an understanding of the technical language of religion, philosophy and theology;
2. Recall basic factual material relevant to the studies involved;
3. Select, use and show understanding of this material;
4. Evaluate primary and secondary sources and to display critical judgment;
5. Construct coherent theological arguments.

The syllabus is in two parts:

Part One is essentially biblical in content. An introduction to biblical literature and critical methods of studying it is followed by the examination in detail of major theological themes as they developed through the biblical period. These centre round the concepts of God and man's response to God in faith, supported by a study of the background notions of sin and salvation and of the community which provides the context for the response in faith.

Part Two is concerned with the live theological development of these concepts, starting with a critical study of the place of philosophical reason in the process. Study then centres on the development of christology as an example of the use of theological reasoning applied to the data of revelation both in the Patristic and contemporary periods, and on the nature of ethics in the light of the New Testament and modern philosophical ideas. Finally the student chooses one major modern theological work in its historical context to study in depth as a means of focussing and applying the theological skills he has acquired.

The final examination will consist of two papers of three hours each based on the two parts of the syllabus. The first paper will be in three Sections, A, B and C; four questions should be attempted, one from each section and a fourth from any section. The second paper will consist of four Sections A, B, C and D; four questions should be attempted, one from each section.

Students may use a Bible in the examination.

PART ONE: BIBLICAL STUDIES

Section A
The Nature of the Bible

The types of literature to be found in the Bible. The authority of the Bible – fundamentalism, revelation, inspiration, the canon. Scripture and Tradition. Critical and historical methods, form, source and redaction criticism. The nature of midrash in the New Testament.

Students will be expected to have considered the following texts, not because of their technical content so much as the problems they raise in relation to the subject matter of this section:
Genesis 1–11; Exodus 20, 34; Deuteronomy 26; Joshua 24; 1 Samuel 7–12; Deuteronomy 5; 1 Samuel 17; 2 Samuel 21 and 23; Psalm 51; 1 Kings 4. 32–34; Ezekiel 34. 23–24. Infancy narratives in Matthew 1–2 and Luke 1–2; Last supper in Mark and John; Resurrection narratives; John 6; Romans 13; 1 Corinthians 7.

Recommended reading (these texts are not examinable, but may be found useful for covering the subject matter being dealt with in this section):
O. Eissfeldt, *The Old Testament, An Introduction*
W. Kummel, *Introduction to the New Testament*
Guthrie, *New Testament Introduction*
C. H. Dodd, *The Authority of the Bible*
Hoskyns and Davey, *The Riddle of the New Testament*
J. Bright, *History of Israel*
F. Filson, *A New Testament History*

Section B
1. The Nature of God

Early animistic and anthropomorphic ideas of God. Yahweh and the covenant. The liberating God of the exodus and exile. Theocracy and monarchy. Eighth century prophets on God. Christ's teaching on his father. Early christology. Spirit.

Texts: Genesis 1–4; Exodus 3, 20; Isaiah 1–6; Amos; Hosea; Colossians, Philippians 2 (these are central texts and are not meant to be exclusive).

Recommended reading:
H. Wheeler Robinson, *Religious Ideas of the Old Testament*
W. Eichrodt, *Theology of the Old Testament*
R. H. Fuller, *Foundations of New Testament Christology*
O. Cullmann, *The Christology of the New Testament*
C. K. Barrett, *The Holy Spirit and the Gospel Tradition*
J. Jeremias, *The Prayers of Jesus*
          The Parables of Jesus

2. Sin and Salvation
Mythic origins of sin. Sin as disobedience to God's law. Sin as origin of suffering and misfortune. Sacrifice as purification from sin. Prophets on sacrifice and repentance. The Messianic tradition. Death and resurrection. Jesus on the forgiveness of sin. New Testament eschatology.

Texts: Genesis 3–11; Exodus 20, 34; Leviticus 16; 2 Samuel 11–12; Psalm 51; Isaiah 52–3; Jonah (and relevant parts of Ezra); Parables in Luke; Miracles in Mark; John 9; Mark 13; 1 Thessalonians 2; 1 Corinthians 15.

Recommended reading:
R. de Vaux, *Ancient Israel*
H. Ringren, *The Messiah in the Old Testament*
H. Wheeler Robinson, op. cit.
W. Manson, *Jesus the Messiah*
J. Jeremias, *New Testament Theology*
R. H. Fuller, *Interpreting the Miracles*
J. Jeremias, *The Parables of Jesus*

Section C

1. The Nature of Faith
Faith as trust in the Old Testament. Prophetic vocation. Faith as commitment in the New Testament – the parables and miracles of Jesus. Discipleship. Faith and justification – sin, death, law and works; salvation according to Paul.

Texts: Genesis 12; Joshua 1, 7; Isaiah 6, 36–39; Jeremiah 1; Ezekiel 1–3; 18; Mark 5; Galatians; Romans 1–8; James; Hebrews 11–12.

Recommended reading:
H. H. Rowley, *The Faith of Israel*
W. Eichrodt, *Old Testament Theology*
G. Ebeling, *The Nature of Faith*
T. W. Manson, *The Teaching of Jesus*
R. Bultmann, *New Testament Theology*

2. The Worshipping Community
Covenant and covenants in the OT Passover festival. Last supper and the eucharist. Baptism and the new covenant. The relationship between theology, liturgy and architecture.

Texts: Genesis 9, 12; Exodus 20, 34; Joshua 24; Deuteronomy 26; 2 Samuel

7; Jeremiah 31; Hebrews 8. 9; Mark 14; John 6, 1; Corinthians 10, 11; Mark 1; John 3; Matthew 28; Acts 15; Romans 6; Galatians 3.

Recommended reading:
W. Eichrodt, *Old Testament Theology*
H. Swanson, *The Kings and Covenant*
R. de Vaux, *Ancient Israel*
O. Cullmann, *Early Christian Worship*
             Baptism in the New Testament
Seasoltz, *The House of God*
E. Schillebeeckx, *The Eucharist*

Part Two: Theological Studies

Section A
The Nature of Religious Belief

A study of the nature of religious belief, religious language and the classical arguments for the existence of God.

Reading:
N. Smart, *Philosophers and Religious Truth*
A. Flew & A. McIntyre (eds), *New Essays in Philosophical Theology*
A. Flew, *God and Philosophy*
I. Ramsey, *Religious Language*
D. Hume, *On Religion*
S. Kierkegaard, *Journals*
J. Bowker, *The Sense of God*

Section B
The Nature of Christ

A study of attempts to understand the nature of Christ, concentrating on the patristic and modern periods.

Reading:
J. N. D. Kelly, *Early Christian Doctrines*
H. Bettensen, *The Early Christian Fathers*
             Documents of the Christian Church
G. Aulen, *Christus Victor*
D. Bonhoeffer, *Christology*
W. Rannenberg, *The Apostles Creed*
J. A. T. Robinson, *The Human Face of God*

Section C
Man and Morality

A consideration of the main ethical theories, philosophical and theological. The student will be expected to show that he can use moral principles in coming to moral decisions about contemporary problems.

Reading:
A. McIntyre, *A Short History of Ethics*
H. McCabe, *Law, Love and Language*
J. Fletcher, *Situation Ethics*
J. Macquarrie, *Three Issues In Ethics*
J. Houlden, *Ethics and the New Testament*
W. Frankena, *Ethics*

Section D
Modern Theology in a Secular Age

Each student will study in detail the ideas of any *one* modern theologian in one major text from the following list. Each text should be studied in the broader context of the ideas and events of its period. Of the titles listed, not more than four may be offered for examination by the School in any one year. The choice of books for examination will be submitted to the Board by the School not later than 30 September each year for the following summer's examination.

The choice of texts should be from the following list:
J. H. Newman, *Essay on the Development of Christian Doctrine*
P. Tillich, *The Courage to Be*
D. Bonhoeffer, *The Cost of Discipleship*
J. Moltmann, *Theology of Hope*
M. Buber, *I and Thou*
H. Küng, *The Church*

NOTES

1. See chapter 8, p. 125.
2. See chapter 1, pp. 25ff.

4 Religious Education in a Monastic Setting
Timothy Wright

This paper, which implicitly questions some of the traditional assumptions behind the denominational school, will aim also to examine some of the perspectives which should influence confessional education today.

Faith and the Christian school

In one sense the crisis over religious education in the confessional school is not simply an educational one, it is also concerned with the nature of faith. We live in a world that looks for quick answers, but none is provided by faith. Because of its nature, faith always produces difficulties, and neither the educational psychologist, nor long experience of teaching can provide formulae for its nurture. Moreover, no amount of religious instruction will produce conviction or commitment. The short answer, which is at the same time the most mysterious, is that faith grows when it encounters faith; but who knows who has faith? Who can spot the faith of another? The cynic will always produce an alternative explanation, and even the qualities associated with faith, like integrity, goodness, generosity, courage and strength of character, can be mistaken during life, or may appear equally strong in the non-believer. This is especially the case in a pluralist and secular age, whose standards and ideals often hinder true discernment. In the last analysis, all that can be said is that men of faith will have influence, and that, in the heart of all, there is a capacity for self-transcendence. The school which accepts both these truths can justify its existence as a denominational school on those grounds alone although the consequences may need further elaboration.

Within the context of the Christian school, this demands an atmosphere in which Christian commitment is positively presented through the attitudes and lives of those involved. This presupposes that all members of the staff recognize and respect the overriding religious commitment of the school although it does not imply a 'spiritual means test' before acceptance. It will stress the need for prayer and worship, while also ensuring that religious studies is structured around the Christian faith. This will not inhibit the inalienable right of each to his point of view, but it will strive to ensure that people are able to provide a rational justification for their own standpoints.

New elements in the 1980s

At the same time, changes in the last twenty years have produced important new elements, which require careful examination, and equally careful application to the educational scene. There are seven such elements that I wish to consider.

1. The renewed emphasis on search or quest

(*a*) The static model of the church is now disintegrating. The same applies in the area of belief, where it is no longer felt that the believer is one who obeys certain rules and holds certain doctrines, while belonging to a definite organization. If scientific advance caused the collapse of the old certainties, today absolute values hold little meaning either. To stand still is to go backwards – progress, change and development are now the key words. The young eschew traditionalism, exemplified in the idea of the church as the stable society in which everything was clear, including ultimate rewards. This means that the security formerly derived from membership of a seemingly stable institution has lost its authenticity. For that reason, organizations which set out to provide ready-made answers, to give rules for behaviour and to pass judgment on attitudes and actions are in danger of being considered irrelevant.

(*b*) The keyword for the new approach is 'search'. Each has to enter upon his own search, and nothing is valid until it has been sought and found. This process of finding is not a final state of certainty, however, but rather a state of provisional living – a pause prior to the next search. Ronald Eyre produced a series of television programmes, entitled 'The Long Search', in which he played the part of the 'searcher', and thus clearly identified himself with the contemporary mood. In November 1980 he commented on this in 'Thought for the Day' as follows:

There is, or so it seems to me, no difficulty in finding talkative people,

who will give you a strong, belligerent line on the teaching of
Jesus, the teaching of the Buddha, of the teaching of the prophet
Mahomet. . .But we found, as we searched, that what we responded
to best was an altogether quieter voice. The voice of Christians whose
Christianity is living a life and not shouting a slogan; of Buddhists
who preach quiet sermons in the way they walk on bare feet; of
Muslims who acknowledge the undivided truth in the grandeur of
God, and prostrate themselves in the face of it. . .

The current attitude towards religion is associated with what is seen
as a search for what is genuine, and this goes deeper than mere emotional
satisfaction. At the same time nothing is regarded as sacrosanct and
unchanging, and even what is 'found' is seen as the starting point for
the next search. Traditional demarcation lines between religions are
less clearly drawn, but this does not mean that a superficial syncretism
is in fashion. What matters is that all who are engaged in the search
should be convinced that there is a point to it, and that there is something
or someone at whom the search is directed. Although definitive statements may be valid for individuals, they are not the short cut to belief
that the searcher needs or desires. In this the meaninglessness of the
alternative is not considered attractive, and atheism acts only as a
temporary intellectual stopping-point. The seeker needs the challenge
of the search, the experience of pain and longing, so that he can fully
enjoy the experience of finding.

This emphasis on personal authentication as the gateway to conviction
leaves the traditional understanding of religious teaching, especially in
denominational schools, in a quandary. The school was established in
order to teach the faith. That entailed instruction in doctrine and morals,
and the provision of occasions for religious practice. It was assumed
that all were believers, and that they intended to remain so. The idea
that a young person could suspend belief, or even doubt whether he
ever had it, was foreign to many educators, though the wise recognized
the difficulties faced by an intelligent person as he grappled with the
problems of scholastic doctrine. Clearly a different type of curriculum
is required if the school is to be an environment for the search or quest.

The implications of this are, to some extent, elucidated by the
experience of the monastic schoolmaster, for whom the search awakens
deeper sentiments. In his rule, St Benedict requires that the novice
should 'truly seek God', (ch. lviii). Cardinal Hume well developed this
idea when trying to answer the question: 'What is the centre of the
monastic calling?'

An exploration into the mystery which is God. A search for an experience of his reality. That is why we become monks. The exploration is a life-long enterprise. And when we come to the end of our lives, the task will not have been completed. Such experience as God will grant you will be a limited, pale thing compared to that for which we are ultimately destined.[1]

If this is true of the monastic life, it is also true of the Christian one. It follows that in recent centuries, where there has been a Christian emphasis on the certainty, security and infallibility of religious truth, it has been misleading.

The element of the search or quest, in religious education, is, in my view, a sufficient justification for monastic schools.

2. The interest in religious experience

The second element, which is the fascination of religious experience as a phenomenon, follows from the first. The search for genuine religious experience in the materialist culture and competitive world of jobs has led to a radical questioning of institutional religion. At the same time, people have tried to investigate the phenomenon of religious experience, and this is exemplified by the establishment at Oxford of the Religious Experience Research Unit. Their publications point to the widespread experience of the Other, or, in other words, of self-transcendence. Alister Hardy writes in the Introduction to Edward Robinson's *The Original Vision*:

> What is important to stress in schools today is that the discussion of religious feelings. . . is no longer to be dominated by conventional ideas of what constitutes religion, or by theological orthodoxies. . .

Edward Robinson himself writes of religious education within our school system, quoting two correspondents:

> 'I do not connect any religious awareness with my school life, which was a happy and normal affair', or again 'I cannot recall that school had any influence at all, religiously, on me, I was just a normal schoolgirl.' These off-hand remarks give the game away so neatly that the point need not be laboured further. It really is a game, education I mean, and the sooner you learn the rules, the easier life will be. 'Schooling, teachers, books – the whole environment – seemed in a completely separate compartment from the development of my religious awareness.' But trying to live at two levels only meant trouble. So 'I deliberately inhibited the inner life and became highly scientific in outlook'. The rest was evidently, from the school's point of view, very successful. If our priorities in education reflect the needs

of what is essentially a competitive society, the kind of competence that our schools will reward will be one that is just not compatible with that slow maturing inner process which is the growth of religious awareness.[2]

This is a crucial point for the denominational schools. Can religious ideals and practices be communicated when the bulk of the curriculum is geared to success in other fields? Or can the very commitment of the teacher, both to his profession and his God, produce an attractive synthesis? The reality of religious awareness cannot now be doubted. What are the structures needed to ensure its growth and development? In his book *Silent Music*, William Johnston writes of the phenomenal growth of meditation in the last two decades – a growth which includes people of all ages, backgrounds and religious ways of life. He says that people are now looking for silence, interiority and religious experience, or, in other words, for contemplation or meditation. Traditional religion has somehow failed such people, because it has been unable to keep pace with the sudden leap in consciousness, which has lead to a more mystical understanding of religion by many people. Those who run denominational schools cannot ignore this. The desire for something beyond surface events and activities, together with widespread experience of such a beyond, suggests that this element must provide part of any renewed curriculum, despite the inherent difficulties.

3. The new understanding of man

From the Second Vatican Council and from John Paul II there has arisen a new understanding of man. This presents a much more positive picture, and less is made of sinfulness, selfish motivation and the evil way of men. This means that, although those things are not denied, a deliberate attempt is made to focus on the positive capacities of man, and, in particular, on his capacity for life with God. On one level, this is a renewed form of sacramental theology, where the indwelling of the Holy Spirit, consequent on baptism, makes each Christian an ikon of the risen Lord (despite the fact that the truth is not always well illustrated by the behaviour of the individuals themselves). The Pastoral Constitution on the Church in the Modern World describes well the confusion of many people about the world, its aims and their own role. The questions asked in section 10 are answered summarily as follows:

> The intellectual nature of man finds at last its perfection, as it should, in wisdom, which gently draws the human mind to look for and to love what is true and good. Filled with wisdom, man is led through visible realities to those which cannot be seen (15).

His conscience is man's most secret core, and his sanctuary. There he is alone with God whose voice echoes in his depths (16).

Man's dignity, therefore, requires him to act out of conscience and free choice, as moved and drawn in a personal way from within, and not by blind impulses in himself, or by mere external constraint (18).

The dignity of man rests above all on the fact that he is called to communion with God. The invitation to converse with God is addressed to man as soon as he comes into being. For if man exists it is because God has created him through love, and through love continues to hold him in existence (19).

The same theme was taken up by Pope John Paul II in his encyclical *Redemptor Hominis* of 1979. He says that God has revealed himself to man in and through Christ, and that through Christ man has gained awareness of his own dignity, and of the surpassing worth of his humanity. The function of the church is seen, in the same encyclical, as being to point the awareness and experience of the whole of humanity to the mystery of God, and to help men to be aware of the redemption taking place in Jesus Christ.

For denominational schools, this presents a challenge, since it raises the question of how these truths are to be taught in the curriculum. How can one challenge the young today to recognize in Jesus Christ the fulfilment of all that is deepest in their nature without making Christ appear as an old fashioned moralizer or an idealist? Examination syllabuses on the Gospel, or the theology of St Paul, can only be part of such a curriculum. Opportunities for prayer, the example of teachers and the values of the school are equally important.

4. Plurality in Christian theology

Another new element is the plurality in Christian theology today. This is important for itself. It is also important because teachers in denominational schools often have difficulty in evaluating the different points of view. The easy way out is to engage in non-judgmental dogmatics. In fact, although it must be recognized that theology is as rigorous and scientific as any other of the humanities, this does pose a problem. The nurture of faith can be seriously affected by critical and unsympathetic academic comment, and this challenges the educators to ensure that theology is well taught. Though that act of ensuring that theology is well taught does involve accepting the pluralism which is a concomitant of true academic rigour, it also involves a recognition of the way in which the life of faith is founded on experience and understanding. In *What is Theology?* Maurice Wiles writes of the way in which variety in theology is not necessarily the fruit of error, and says that different theologies may be complementary to one another rather than in competition. Such variety may help theology to move towards its goal, which is infinitely greater than human understanding – namely God himself.

With direct relevance to education, the same point is made in a different way by one of my monastic brethren, Father Aelred Graham. Writing of the Catholic educator in the 1961 *Harvard Educational Review*, he says:

> He will not state one side of the case only; for that would be un-Catholic; since 'catholic' is a Greek word meaning 'according to the whole'. If, however, out of his devotion to the truth, without special pleading, or forcing the note, he happened to say something rather more luminous than most of his contemporaries are saying, that also, I would think, might emerge from the nature of the case. But here we should be above the level of sectarian controversy – shouldn't we? Because truth is not *for* or *against* anything. Truth simply is.

More challengingly, in *The End of Religion* he writes, at a deeper level, of an ecumenism of the spirit. While this might not make differences of church organization disappear, it might mean that people would come to see that they do not matter very much. This discovery depends on a deeper religious understanding, however; one which puts verbal formulae and theological speculations into perspective.

5. The role of commitment in religious studies teaching

It is necessary, at this point, to juxtapose the views considered in Schools Council *Working Paper 36* and those of Dr Edward Hulmes. The Working Paper considers the view of Lawrence Stenhouse, Director of the Schools Council/Nuffield Foundation Humanities Curriculum project. He sees the teacher as an impartial chairman, who should see that all relevant viewpoints are fairly considered.

> This will include his own view, but he should arrange for this to be introduced as one among many opinions, put forward by someone else, perhaps from a book or newspaper cutting. . .

It is suggested in the Working Paper that this is an approach which a teacher would do well to adopt for a few weeks, even if it is not part of a professional code. It is felt that this will make the teacher both more sensitive to the dialogue between his pupils, and conscious of the effect of his own intervention. This section of the Working Paper concludes by saying:

Education thrives on the airing of conflicting viewpoints in a common desire to let truth prevail. However, truth stands little chance of emerging from this conflict if one view is armed with a howitzer while the rest have only pea-shooters and catapults!

If such a view can be sympathetically accepted when it is seen as a way of safeguarding RE teachers from the accusation of indoctrination, it may also lead to the implication that the experience of the RE teacher is a disadvantage in the classroom. Of this Edward Hulmes writes that the teacher's commitment is explicitly the primary resource out of which religious education flows, and by which it is nourished and developed.

> There are two primary requirements. In the first place. . . the teacher will have brought his own religious commitment to an advanced degree of self-conscious awareness. Without this. . .he has clearly not begun to take seriously the educational resource of his own religious belief. . . The second requirement is to recognize that religious education is a dynamic activity at its best, and that some means must be found whereby his own commitment becomes not only more self-conscious but self-critical.[3]

This point is further developed by Kenneth Wilson in his paper. It is also in accord with earlier remarks about the need for search, while recognizing that the RE teacher's search cannot be impartial with regard to its obligation or end. Indeed there is a danger if a clearly defined content based on revealed truth, or at least corporate experience, is not presented as a challenge to the young. Doctrine cannot be well taught if it is done 'impartially'. Although it requires a respect for freedom, it also requires a respect for conviction.

6. The need for academic RS in the sixth form

There are three main advantages in having religious studies taught as a full academic subject in the sixth form.

First, it provides a framework for the course, which gives to the teacher and pupil clear objectives, and so avoids the reduction of these lessons to superficial discussion, where unresponsive audiences discourage the over-worked teacher in his efforts to go further. Moreover a clear structure gives incentives to the teacher as well as to the taught, which makes proper teaching possible, while avoiding the personalized 'witness' approach, which, if popular at one time, is often greeted with cynicism and resentment.

Secondly, the well ordered content of academic RS courses provides an opportunity for a deeper study and understanding of religion. Where a variety of options is available, specialization is possible, and further research encouraged.

Thirdly, the material covered in an academic RS course touches the fundamental questions of human life. Through the rigour of a course that is properly academic, the young are trained to think more maturely, and to be critical of the platitudes purveyed through the media and elsewhere. Moreover, it is to be expected that such a method would illustrate the dangers for a true understanding of a religion of sentimental piety and uncritical rationalism alike.

It is no longer possible to teach religious studies at sixth form level in a dogmatic and personalist way, since the results are counter-productive. It is important that there should be a variety of academic courses, taught with that blend of objectivity, enthusiasm and commitment which is essential for true education.

7. Religious studies and the future

The final element in the educational scene concerns the purpose of education in a world of technological change. This is not simply a political problem, for, in essence, it is human, moral and religious. It involves each person in facing up to himself, and undertaking a journey inward. E. F. Schumacher has written that the modern attempt to live without religion has failed, and that the requirement now is a *metanoia* or turning round. In that way the world may be seen in a new light, as a place where there can be enough food, and where men have the competence to provide the necessities, which would mean that no one need live in misery. If this is to be achieved, it requires the best method of education.

> Love, empathy, *participation mystique*, understanding, compassion; these are the faculties of a higher order than those required for the implementation of any policy of discipline or freedom. To mobilise these higher faculties or forces, to have them available not simply as occasional impulses, but permanently; that requires a higher level of self-awareness, and that makes a great educator.[4]

For us in the denominational sector changes will place more, not less, emphasis on religious education both in the strictly academic context, and, perhaps, more emphatically, as part of the other elements in education, particularly in boarding schools.

Summary

These then, are the seven important factors of our educational world: the replacement of institution by search, the growth of meditation at the expense of formal worship, the new awareness of man, the increase of pluralism in theology, the role of commitment in religious education, the need for academic RS, and the challenges presented by the developments in technology. The most significant feature that they illustrate is the need for a real spiritual dimension in education. The search must be undertaken as a journey that will involve contemplation, while the arguments of theology must be subject to the recognition that all language is limited in expressing truth and the search for it.

The problems of what is termed 'indoctrination' are overcome by recognizing the inner freedom of each individual, and schools must recognize that this primacy of conscience is constitutive of a person's dignity. Within that recognition a radical *metanoia* must be sought, which reverses the values of self-importance and success. If this challenge faces all denominational schools, it is particularly important in those boarding schools that are run by religious. The monk should delight in this, for it spells the end of the scientific hegemony, and the frenetic competition for secular success, though perhaps these have always been more important to the educators than the educated. The drive to produce a successful school and to gain pupils has too often overridden the genuine insights which the monastic vocation brings to ordinary human and Christian living.

A note by Dom Christopher Jamison, Head of Religious Education at Worth School

This symposium took as its starting point the difference between two approaches to theology (see Introduction). The first approach is descriptive, proceeding inductively to examine the experience of life and its meaning. The second approach is deductive, investigating a scheme of religious doctrine in its own right. This note aims to show that these two approaches are complementary and that confessional schools have a unique role to play in developing a complete religious education involving a new synthesis.

For a variety of reasons, the descriptive[5] study of religion has become the new orthodoxy in many schools. This method is concerned with the observable activities of religion, such as history, buildings, pilgrimages and the phenomena of experience such as conflict, suffering, death. As a reaction to this, many confessional schools either produced a more sophisticated catechetical approach or made Christianity itself the object of phenomenological study. Catechesis or phenomenology are not the only alternatives, however.

Confessional schools are in a unique position to help students to examine not just the 'phenomena' of religion, but also what we might call the 'noumena'[6] of religion; faith, the incarnation of the Beyond in our midst, the renewal of life through the Spirit, liberation. It is here that real Christian faith operates. Real religious language is not a description but an exploration of these things. The description of phenomena and the investigation of doctrine are both needed, but both alike need the sense of exploring the vital, transcendent being of God and of Man.

The reality of faith, which the early fathers called 'the mysteries', lies hidden[7] in the life and history of the religious community. Religious education should try to point to these hidden things. This community is the given reality which the student is asked to explore. It is not just a conveniently placed cage or laboratory into which the student is asked to peer. Though formal or sacramental entry into it is not the direct concern of the classroom, the student may properly be asked to empathize with the religious community.

As in the study of literature, some belief in beauty is necessary, so in the study of religion, some belief in the transcendent is also necessary. Tearing a poem to pieces or reading it with no enjoyment both destroy literary appreciation. So too the appreciation of religion requires a belief in its reality.[8] The confessional school, especially the monastic school, offers a unique opportunity for that. In the classroom, the customs, lifestyle and history of the local community (parish or monastery) can be a way into describing the realities of faith and commitment which underlie them. A teacher can describe the place of the Eucharist in his own life.[9] A monastery can offer a chance to share in its common life, its prayer and its compassion.

Classroom and community can form a single fabric, blending the phenomena and noumena. The pupil in a monastic school, for example, has a chance to examine and to join in the monk's search for God. That this chance can be made available need imply no constraint on the pupil to accept the faith presented, and so reflects modern educational requirements. This approach also offers a complete view of religion as living faith, and, as such, does the greatest possible justice to the real nature of religion itself.

NOTES

1. Basil Hume, *Searching for God*, Hodder 1977, ch. 2, p. 28.
2. Edward Robinson, *The Original Vision*, Oxford, Manchester College, Religious Experience Research Unity 1977, p. 79.
3. Edward Hulmes, *Commitment and Neutrality in Religious Education*, Geoffrey Chapman 1979, pp. 90f.
4. E. F. Schumacher, *A Guide for the Perplexed*, Abacus 1978, p. 143.
5. See chapter 8, p. 127.
6. See chapter 8, p. 123.
7. See chapter 6, p. 97.
8. See chapter 11, p. 159.
9. See Edward Hulmes, op. cit., pp. 90f.

5 Religious Education and Theology in the Anglican Independent School

James Barnett

Despite their Christian heritage, the time given to chapel services, and the provision of 'divinity' periods, there is no tradition of theological education in the Anglican independent school. The extent to which this is true is demonstrated by two things written half a century ago. In 1936, in a volume of essays called *The Headmaster Speaks*, J. T. Christie of Repton wrote:

> Any attempt to give a new emphasis to religion in Public Schools is apt to meet with the objection from school-masters of experience that English schoolboys are shy of religion, at any rate religion of a theological kind.

Similarly, in Arnold Lunn's *Public School Religion* (1933), the Rev. Dr C. A. Allington, Headmaster of Eton, wrote that he had a horror of experts of all kinds, and profoundly disliked the idea that religion was a matter on which only the clergy had a right to speak. He went on to say:

> We are not blind to the fact that our method involves the risk of bad teaching, given in a perfunctory way, but we feel that we gain the services of many men who would never describe themselves as expert, and yet are admirable teachers of Divinity.

For Hugh Lyon in *The Headmaster Speaks*, scripture teaching was not a 'necessary subject' since it was not examinable, although it was essential to a boy's 'general development'!

Such an attitude was responsible for the decline of RE. As the broader curriculum replaced the classical one with subjects relevant to the modern world and syllabuses aimed at examinations, neither teachers nor taught could continue to regard 'divinity' as a serious subject. In the years after the Second World War, however, many schools (among them Uppingham and Repton) redressed the balance by arranging that scripture should be studied for O level.

Here was an extra subject and an 'easy pass' for pupil and teacher alike. For the teacher, no specialist knowledge of theology was required, and form-masters could teach the syllabus. For the pupil, there was no need to demonstrate those qualities of serious thought and discernment demanded elsewhere in the curriculum. For example, in the summer of 1959, candidates were required only to retell some of the stories of St Mark's Gospel, and to study the history of the Northern Kingdom from the rise of the House of Omri to the fall of the House of Jehu. It followed that there was little esteem for the subject on the part of anyone involved, so that pressure on the O level timetable from other subjects, like science, meant that divinity was an obvious target. Moreover, and perhaps more important, as the ethos of the schools began to change in the late fifties, so did the attitude to religious teaching.

In 1961, Canon J. B. Goodliffe, who had been Rector of Cheltenham, and one of the chaplains at Cheltenham College, wrote, in his book *School Chaplain*, about what he termed the 'revolution in Divinity'. He said that this took the form of a change from the academic to the dynamic, which meant that all problems must be assessed in the light of the gospel. Moreover, he rejected the idea of the scripture lesson, which he felt should be replaced by teaching the faith in close alliance with the worship of the church. He also felt that there were more important events to study than the violence and brutality of early tribal chieftains. For example, the rising tide of nationalism could only be countered by the work of missionaries who proclaimed the inter-nationalism of God: 'St Paul's missionary journeys have a real value, not as travelogues, but as the foundation of the universal character of the church.' The history of the last ten years has shown the failure of this method, as well, as a means of teaching the young about Christianity or religion.

The reasons for this failure deserve further consideration. From an academic point of view, it is clear that the approach advocated by Canon Goodliffe lacks rigour. Nevertheless it does point to a degree of Christian witness and service not readily apparent to those who were required to engage only in learning the biblical text so as to regurgitate its contents in their own words for an examiner. Such a tradition of service, and of attempted reconciliation between different people has marked the expressed aims of the schools in the past century, as witness the establishment of clubs and settlements in large towns, of which the

Repton Club in Bethnal Green is an example. The lack of academic rigour notwithstanding, the widespread failure of the schools to take Canon Goodliffe's approach seriously on any but the smallest of scales is worthy of remark.

In this area, economic pressures have been of paramount importance, and the aspiration of contemporary society, or more particularly, of a section of it, has determined the nature of parental requirements. As anyone who has advised the young on their choice of career will know, careers with social cachet, highly regarded by society, and preferably well paid, are almost always preferred to those which are less fashionable, but for which there may be a real need. The probation service is an example of this. When these parental requirements are allied to the pressure of examinations and the need for qualifications, the effect on the ethos and atmosphere within the schools is profound.

In recent years, when fees have risen faster than parental incomes, the schools have remained more or less full because of their success in providing what the paymasters – the parents – want. The favourable ratio of teachers to pupils, careful and dedicated teaching all day and well into the night and, no less important, the pressures exerted by teachers both on and through their pupils, have enabled young people to gain qualifications which, with their several abilities, they would not have gained elsewhere. The effect of this has been exemplified by the attitude of pupils to their teachers, particularly in and after their O level year. Masters are praised or criticized in the light of the results of those whom they teach. They are expected to feed their pupils, often with the metaphorical spoon, with the material of the examination syllabus, and to give them the skills with which they may impress examiners. For the parent and pupil, this is at least as important as more properly educational considerations. It is not only in shops that the customer is always right.

Despite the desirability of competence and success, the extent of this emphasis indicates a significant tension between the expressed ideals of the schools, and the work which they are actually required to do. If this is partly the result of simple economic pressure, it is also the result of the materialism of recent years, exemplified by the slogan ascribed to Mr Macmillan, 'You've never had it so good', by Mr Wilson's technological revolution, and even, dare one say it, by an inflexible devotion to monetarist economic theory. If, in the early sixties, Canon Goodliffe's revolution in divinity seemed to point to a means of reconciliation, the passage of the years has shown the fallacy of that argument.

It follows that a paper which called only for more and better RE would be aimed at the wrong target. It would be one among many voices aimed at improving the teaching of different subjects in the curriculum, and it would in no wise bridge the gap which exists between the Christian's quest for God or for the meaning and purpose of life and the current aspirations of many of those who have achieved the degree of success in the secular world which makes it possible for them to pay independent school fees. If RE is to be regarded as of real value in the independent school, the nature of the difference between the aspirations of parents and children, and truly Christian insights must be clearly understood.

Such an understanding demands a revolution, since parents do not have Christian values in mind when they choose an independent school and pay the fees. Indeed the headmaster of one famous public school said that, in five years, he was not asked a single question by prospective parents about chapel or religious education. It follows that a deductive approach, aimed at imparting Christian values, can hardly expect an enthusiastic reception. Moreover, and this is more important, there is a very significant sense in which the economic basis of these schools, and the concomitant requirement of worldly success, places them at variance with the Christianity which they profess. If the degree of variance is to be reduced, and the revolution to be achieved, the onus for the achievement is on the religious educator.

The task of the educator, and the reason why he must seek a more sophisticated approach, which does not presume Christian understanding, can be further refined. The fact that the public schools are at variance with the Christianity which they profess points to the nature of their profession. When Canon Goodliffe wrote of the difference between the rising tide of nationalism and the internationalism of God, he exemplified the problem. It is both deceptively and misleadingly easy to claim religious justification for widely accepted secular conduct. In this century, the role of the church in time of war demonstrates this. In the First World War a poster taken from the Christmas 1914 number of the *Graphic*,[1] and hung in many churches deliberately likened the sacrifice of the soldier to that of Christ, and implied that God was on the British side. More recently the conflict over the Falkland Islands Service has raised questions about such easy assumptions. By implication, that latter debate has pointed to the way in which one who is truly committed to the search must question assumptions in many areas. Essentially secular institutions will always be disturbed when Christianity is taught in such terms, and they are not likely to embrace it with much enthusiasm.

If true religion is to gain a hearing, therefore, religious education in school must be an academic subject, taught in classroom time, and enabled to demonstrate its respectability and rigour for itself. That applies neither more nor less to independent schools than others, and it need not be an exclusively Christian virtue. Such religious education must be as theological as history is historical and mathematics is mathematical. The content and method of study must show a real awareness of the work currently being done by academic theologians, so that, in the secular world, the educational as opposed to the ecclesiastical justification for RE may be understood. The argument which justifies RE in the curriculum must be based on the need for children to understand the spiritual experience of man, rather than on the suggestion that they absorb the teaching of the church.

Let me illustrate this from my own experience. I went to Uppingham in 1972 in a climate of opinion following hot on the heels of the sixties, which had emphasized the role of the RE teacher as chaplain and counsellor, at the expense of his function as a theologian. Even so, I was somewhat surprised when five out of the first seven classes that I took expected the lesson to be a discussion of pornography. Since, however, I had already taught for a number of years, I was no longer so naive as to expect a subject taught on one period a week throughout the school to be taken seriously.

My first priority was to encourage my pupils to see the RE teacher's function as the theological one in which I believed. Therefore, I turned my attention to O level, which had previously been done only by a very small number of people in their spare time; and that without any great success. The result was that, in the Lent and Summer terms, I had a class of more than twenty people for three properly timetabled periods each week. The course went well, the pupils enjoyed it, and the results were very satisfactory.

The syllabus set by the Oxford and Cambridge Board consisted of the Gospel according to St Mark, the Sermon on the Mount, the parables of the kingdom in Matthew 13, and Luke 14–16. Though too high a proportion of the marks, in my view, was given for a simple regurgitation of the text, it was possible, in teaching, to give some knowledge of the background of the New Testament, and the development of its material, so that the class understood better the texts of the Bible, which, in those days, they already knew. I also had small groups, of two and three respectively, starting their A level courses in each of my first two years.

In the long term, however, although Uppingham as a school, and the Director of Studies and the Headmaster in particular, were generous and helpful in making possible the provision in the time-table of periods for public exams, I still had to work hard at demonstrating the academic respectability of theology in school. When I asked, at a Heads of Departments meeting for an extra period in the fifth form, my colleagues were united in refusing to give up time to the subject for which least provision was made. Indeed, one who was prominent in the local church was at pains to point out that it would for ever be impossible for the head of RE to have his subject taken seriously, and that I would do well to accept that.

In my second year at Uppingham, however, my pupils still enjoyed their O level course, and said that they wished to continue the subject. Since, however, some of them wanted to be doctors, and the parents of others did not regard theology as a proper academic discipline, they did not wish to do A level. At the same time, and this is more important, I was not prepared to allow them to do it either. I took the decision to have no more A level sets because, although the grades of my pupils were quite satisfactory in comparison with their achievements in other subjects, they did not regard the syllabus, as then constituted, as properly academic. They felt that the questions in the exam were too closely related to the text of the Bible, rather than to its context (for example in the theological development of the apostolic church), for it to compare favourably with what they did in English or other subjects.

At the same time, and this had more serious implications, they felt that a syllabus which more or less ignored the two millennia of Christian history to which I and they were heirs was incomplete. By their questions in class, and the not uninteresting discussion which ensued, it was clear that they had hoped that A level RE would lead to serious thought about those issues of the meaning of life, and the search for truth, of which they were becoming increasingly aware.

The given syllabus represented a method of RE which had been acceptable to many teachers, and especially those in independent schools, since the days of the school certificate. By the early seventies, however, ready access to foreign travel, developments in the media, increasing choice in society at large, and the simple fact that young people matured earlier had produced a different attitude to religion. In particular, my pupils were not only asking more sophisticated questions about sin, salvation or justice, but they were also adopting a more open approach than their predecessors – one that did not take the answers of traditional Christianity for granted. This was more redolent of what they did in other subjects; it was also not dissimilar from the attitude of adults, who have come to appreciate that the questions with which religion is concerned have many facets. Moreover, the events of the sixties had eroded the institutional role of the school, and with it, that enforced prolongation of adolescence, which had still been an obvious result of independent school education when we went up to universities in the early years of that decade.

For those reasons I agreed with the O level set that we would do an AO level in Church History in the lower sixth. The period was 1972 to the present day, and the Oxford and Cambridge Board set a special paper. My aim was that those who did the course should have some intelligent insight into the development of ideas in the period involved, so that they could see something of the role of the church in society, and of the way in which theological ideas develop. That course normally attracted about ten people, who, in addition to finding it interesting and enjoyable, also discovered that theology was a 'proper' subject. At that stage, also, the first of my pupils, who was a non-ordinand, decided to read theology at university, and went up to Keble College, Oxford. He was the first of a small, but steady number. They demonstrated both the academic respectability of theology, and, which is tactically important, its usefulness as a means of increasing the statistical level of achievement by the school. It should be added to the last point that, as in any other area of knowledge, some people are good at theology when they are not good at other things. Theology is not a soft option!

It was because of this AO course that, at the beginning of 1977, Timothy Wright got in touch with me. He had just become senior RS master at Ampleforth, and, like me, he was anxious that the subject should have academic respectability. Since he also wanted to do a Church History paper, the Oxford and Cambridge Board suggested that he should write to me, and that we should make the paper a common one.

The result was not only that we agreed to collaborate over the Church History, but also that we held a meeting at Ampleforth, at which we drew up an A level syllabus on the *Theology of the Church and Sacraments*. It was well received by pupils, both at Ampleforth and Uppingham, and is now being more widely taken up. The syllabus is concerned with the theology of initiation, the Eucharist and the church in the first six centuries, in the Reformation period, and in the modern period. As such it represents a systematic study of the development and nature of Christian doctrine, and its method is designed to enable people, regardless of their standpoint, to investigate the growth of Christian thought, and the meaning of Christian language.[2] They can see the logical progression of ideas, and the cohesiveness of Christian belief. At the same time, whatever their own view, they may come to see that what they are studying arose as a result of what people believed to be their experience of the spirit of God. Thus the believer may see more of what is involved, and the non-believer may come to a sympathetic understanding of belief. Brenda Watson has more to say about this in her paper, and the principle is an important one, since it is central to the secular justification for teaching theology in the academic timetable. Although different people have their own ideas about courses and syllabuses, which depend upon the books they have read, the interests of their former teachers, and the university to which they went, I do wish to emphasize the importance of the method involved in this syllabus. It seems to me that this is an admirable way of enabling the positive questioning of the sixth former to be guided towards an appreciation of the subtlety of theology.

At this point, the academic competence on which the school depends for its success, and the theologian for his discipline, merge. The part of the argument which applies to all schools is complete, and its relevance to the Anglican independent one implicit. At the same time, and this is more important, a prognosis about the probable nature of the task of independent schools in the years to come, raises fundamental issues. The impact of changes in technology will produce conditions, both in education and society, whose discontinuity with the past will be greater than any previous revolution.

In this the product of the independent school will be particularly vulnerable. As the Mini-Metro, or that hero of advertisements a few years ago, the Fiat Strada are 'handbuilt by robots', so also many of the tasks required in the careers to which pupils in independent schools have traditionally looked forward will be taken over by machines. In particular, basic, but quite highly skilled organizational tasks, such as the control of stock and supplies, and even quite involved accountancy, will be performed by machines based on the micro-processor. With proper programming, the machines neither forget, nor do they make mistakes, so that, as the manual dexterity of the factory worker is being taken over by the robot, the mental dexterity of people of considerable ability will be taken over by machine intelligence.

Although there are many uncertainties about future developments, it is certain that the difference between skill and creativity will be thrown into starker contrast than ever before. Despite the cacophony of electronic music, we are assured by those who understand these things that the difference in nature between human and machine intelligence is such that machines will never become really great writers, artists or composers. It is in the area of their skills, rather than their creativity, therefore, that people are threatened. The implication of this for the independent school is that precisely those people for whom such schools have been most useful in the past will have to reconsider their future prospects.

The success of these schools in enabling people to pass examinations, mentioned earlier, has depended on careful instruction, and on the imparting of skills and techniques. Although some have objected that the advantage has been unfair, and although the secular pressures on the schools are at variance with their Christian tradition, this is one more among countless privileges in the history of the world that have been obtained with money. In the future, however, *really* good jobs, in the management and control of industry for example, will only be available for those with the highest intelligence, and that precludes two thirds or three quarters of pupils in independent schools.

Traditionally these people, like nearly all other members of society, have found occupation at any rate, and, one hopes, fulfilment and purpose in their chosen careers. In the future, whatever the precise nature of the patterns that will emerge, education will have to prepare people to find those things in spheres of activity radically different from those to which most parents and children currently look forward. For this it will be necessary to foster creative ability, so that people may be of interest to themselves and others. This will lead to an enforced reassessment of the value of work, and of the way in which the performance of tasks essential to the common weal has, until recently, been held to impart dignity to man. This must also lead to a reexamination of the doctrine of the person, and of what it means to say that man is a spiritual being made in the image of God. If practical expression is to be given to the unique worth of the individual, and if such expression is to be acceptable to society at large, the materialist goals of all sectors of the educational system, but especially of the independent one, will require radical reassessment.

In this area, the independent schools are well placed to make a real contribution to society in the future, because of the things which they do best. Articulate children, from homes where conversation plays an important part, should be expected to have made such a start in terms of reading, cultural pursuits and experience as to be able to see the value of a creative contribution to mankind, rather than of one which is aimed primarily at material advancement. Moreover, the schools themselves, with large staffs, musical, artistic and other facilities, and, what has been said earlier notwithstanding, traditions of service and leadership, are more than averagely well placed to help their pupils to see the importance of this, and to pursue it.

Insight into the spiritual nature of man, and into the meaning and purpose of life, however partial they must be in this world, will require people who are truly committed to the search or quest for truth. It will also require people who have been helped by their education to engage in that search as intelligently as possible. For this good theology will be essential to the curriculum. Moreover, because of the pressing need for *re*assessment and *re*examination, this approach will have to be newer, more radical and more rigorous than is compatible with a traditionalist authority imposed by either church or school. Paradoxically this process is the one most likely to ensure the survival of the independent school, since it will ensure the value of its product to society in the future, and so obtain in the future a position which approximates as nearly as possible to the one for which the clientele has traditionally paid.

This element of selection creates difficulty for Christians, since it carries the implication that position and status in society are, in some sense, available for purchase. It also raises the question of how far a school with this as one of its principles of selection may regard itself as a Christian one, whatever the terms of the foundation. Indeed, for precisely that reason some of the best of contemporary Anglican clergy eschew the offer of posts in Anglican public schools, or the suggestion that they should apply for them.

For the teacher of religious education in the classroom, the problem may be seen in the following light. The education given in these schools is a good one. Its quality, in terms both of academic efficiency and of the way in which pupils are prepared to serve society, is demonstrated by the high number of public school old boys and girls in positions of responsibility. That number is many times greater than their proportion in society as a whole. If theology is important in education, it is important in these schools. Indeed, implicit in what has been said earlier is the contention that good RE is essential if the best traditions of service and leadership are to be made available by pupils from these schools to their fellow men. If RE is not well done in these schools, there is a consequently greater danger that the more totally materialist aims of parents and their children will increase the divisions which already exist in society. Either RE is essential to a complete curriculum or it is not. If it is essential, it is certainly essential to the independent schools, and a symposium which is concerned with schools of all types would be defective if it did not consider the work of the theologian in the independent school.

APPENDIX

The Theology of the Church and Sacraments

This syllabus is available as one of the options, at A level, from the Oxford and Cambridge Schools Examination Board. The examination consists of two three hour papers, of which this may be one. It may be taken with any of the other options currently available.

The syllabus, of which details are given below, consists of set texts, from which passages may be chosen for comment or discussion, in addition to prescribed areas of study.

In the examination paper, questions *one* and *two* are compulsory. In both questions, passages are set for comment or discussion. In question *one* the passages are selected from the biblical material, and in question *two* from the non-biblical material. The other questions are essay questions, from which candidates make their selection in such a way that they must demonstrate a reasonable breadth of knowledge.

The biblical material prescribed for detailed textual study is as follows:

Matt. 10, 16, 18, 28	I Cor. 1, 11, 12.
Mark 4, 14.1–31	Gal. 3, 4, 5.
Luke 3, 22.1–38	Eph. 2, 3, 4
John 3, 6	I Tim. 3
Acts 2, 8, 19, 20	Heb. 7
Rom. 6	I Peter 2.1–17

Much of the non-biblical material is available in *Documents of the Christian Church*, selected and edited by Henry Bettenson, OUP 1967. Where appropriate the page numbers are given for ease of reference.

The non-biblical material is as follows:

Didache: VII, IX, X, XI, XII, XIII, XIV, XV (Bettenson, pp. 64–6).
  Church Order
Cyprian: De Unitate: iv–vii (Bettenson, pp. 71–73).
  On the Episcopate: Epistle xxxiii:1 and Ep. lxvi:7 (Bettenson, pp. 73–4).
Hippolytus: Ap. Trad: The Liturgy of Hippolytus (Bettenson, pp. 75–6).
Luther: The Babylonish Captivity of the Church On Sacraments (Bettenson, pp. 197–9).
Calvin: The Institute of the Christian Religion: Book II: i, iv; Book III: xxi; Book IV: xiv, xvii (Bettenson, pp. 213–4).

The Prayer of Consecration from the Service of Holy Communion in the Book of Common Prayer of 1662.
The Roman Canon of the Tridentine Mass.
The following of the Thirty-Nine Articles:
  xix: Of the Church.

xxv: Of the sacraments.

xxvi: Of the Unworthiness of Ministers, which hinders not the effect of the Sacrament.

xxvii: Of Baptism

xxviii: f the Lord's Supper.

xxix: Of the Wicked which eat not the Body of Christ in the use of the Lord's Supper.

xxx: Of both kinds.

xxxi: Of the one Oblation of Christ finished upon the Cross.

The Council of Trent:

Canons on Justification: Session VI: January 1547: (Bettenson, p. 263).

On the Eucharist: Session XIII: October 1551.

Chapter IV: On Transubstantiation.

Chapter V: On the worship and veneration of the Holy Eucharist. Canons on the Holy Eucharist (Bettenson, p. 264).

The following passages from the ARCIC Statements:

The Windsor Statement on the Eucharist (1971): Sections 5, 6 & 8.

The Venice Statement on Authority (1976): Sections 1, 5, 12, 15 & 18.

The Canterbury Statement on Ministry (1973): Sections 3, 7, 13 & 16.

The Syllabus

Section I: The Church

(*a*) Church Organization and Government in the First Six Centuries.
- the development of the episcopate and priesthood.
- the growth of papal authority.
- the role of other gifts in the church.

(*b*) The Reformation Objectives.
- the Reformers and their attitude to the priesthood, bishops and the Pope.
- the nature of the church in Reformation theology.
- the RC reform of the church following the Council of Trent.
- Papal infallibility as defined in Vatican I.

(*c*) The Understanding of the Church Today.
- the ecumenical movement and the understanding of the church.
- new developments within the RC Church following Vatican II.
- the understanding of authority within the church today.
- the insights and advances in the Agreed Statements on Ministry and Authority.

Section II: Baptism and Justification

(*a*) Baptism in the Early Church.
- baptism in the New Testament.

- the development of the Rites of Initiation in the first six centuries.
- the problems surrounding infant baptism.

(b) Justification and Grace during the Reformation Period.
- Luther and Calvin on Justification.
- the Council of Trent on Justification.
- the problem of Predestination.

(c) Justification Today.
- new understanding concerning natural and supernatural.
- the Ecumenical significance.
- the theology of grace today.

Section III: The Eucharist
(a) The Eucharist in the Early Church.
- the role and understanding of the Eucharist in the early church.
- the development of the eucharistic liturgy to the sixth century.
- the theology of the early Canons.

(b) The Eucharist during the Reformation Period.
- the Roman Catholic understanding of the Real Presence.
- the objections of the Reformers.
- the Reforms of the Liturgy: the Book of Common Prayer and the Tridentine Mass.

(c) the Modern Problems concerning the Eucharist.
- the reforms of the Liturgy – Rite A, and the Missa Normativa.
- the theology of the Windsor Agreement.
- current problems concerning the Real Presence.

The AO Level Syllabus

The development of the AO level syllabus took place over a period of about five years. The importance of this syllabus is that it demonstrates the influence of the monastic setting, the difficulties experienced by young people in understanding the real nature of adult spirituality, and the need for syllabuses to introduce people to a method of study which does not have to be unlearned.

The examination consists of a three hour paper, in which five questions must be answered. The original development of the syllabus was basically historical. Nevertheless, by the inclusion of such topics as Science and Religion, Biblical Criticism, and some aspects of the difficulties faced by the church in relation to totalitarian regimes, it aimed to help pupils to see that there is a continual process of development in theology, and that this process is related to factors outside the church. The topics were also chosen so that doctrinal issues could be examined.

The twelve topics of the syllabus were as follows:
1. The Early Anglican Evangelicals to 1840.

2. The Oxford Movement and the Anglo-Catholic tradition to *Lux Mundi*.
3. Science and Religion: 1850–1870 & 1950–1970.
4. Biblical Criticism and its impact in Nineteenth-Century England and Germany.
5. The Roman Catholic Church in England in the Nineteenth Century.
6. The First Vatican Council (1870).
7. Catholic Modernism in England and on the Continent.
8. The Second Vatican Council.
9. The Ecumenical Movement and the World Council of Churches, and Ecumenism.
10. Missionary Movements in the Nineteenth Century.
11. Christian Social Thought in the Twentieth Century.
12. The Church and Nazism, Fascism and Communism.

Later development entailed slight modification of these areas of study, and added a number of topics, which were concerned with prayer and spirituality. It was not expected that every area of the syllabus would be covered in the course of a year, but it was hoped that the spread of questions would make the broader syllabus both teachable and examinable. The course was followed for some time at Ampleforth, and very good work was done during the year. Other schools involved have expressed misgivings about the capacity of people in their mid teens to cope adequately with some of the topics, and tend to teach more nearly to the original syllabus.

The topics of the extended syllabus are given here. Since not much work has been attempted in this field, it is of more than historical interest. In the immediate future, however, it is likely that interest will be focussed on the twelve topics of the earlier syllabus.

The Extended Syllabus:

1. The Churches after the Revolution in France
   – Church of England – recent history in the British Isles.
   – Roman Catholic Church – on the continent, especially France, Germany, Italy and Holland.

2. The Evangelicals
   – definition: reasons for revival: lay and clerical involvement; influence on parliament; reforming social moves; assessment.

3. The Oxford Movement until Newman became a Catholic
   – definition: high church tradition and theology; aims in 1830s, theology and politics.
   – role of Newman, Froude, Keble and Pusey: Reasons for Newman's conversion.

4. Pius IX and Vatican I
   – aims of Pontificate: centralization of authority.

– unification of Italy – new dogmatism of papacy – Quanta Cura – Immaculate conception.

– background to the Council; parties in the Church; Dei Filius and Pastor Aeternus; consequences of infallibility.

– note on French liberal Catholicism.

5. The growth of the Catholic Church in England to the Death of Manning
   – penal times; Cxviii revival; Irish Famine.
   – converts; restoration of the hierarchy; new climate.
   – Manning and Newman; Newman as theologian; Manning's leadership.

6. Catholic Modernism
   – background; general features of the movement.
   – Loisy; Lagrange; von Hugel; Tyrrell; Italian Modernists.
   – condemnation of modernism and effects.

7. The Nineteenth Century Missionary Movement to 1910
   – origins and causes, ideals and methods.
   – RC and Protestant missions in China, India and Africa.
   – comparison in methods and achievement.
   – Carey, Taylor, Lavigerie, Livingstone.

8. The Modern Papacy
   – Leo XIII – liberalizing policies; Pius X and anti-modernism.
   – Benedict XV; papacy and politics.
   – Pius XI: relation with Fascism; advances in social teaching.
   – Pius XII – attitude to papacy and war; centralization.
   – John XXIII and Paul VI – contrast in styles of contemporary popes.

9. Ecumenical Movement from 1910
   – growth of World Council of Churches; assemblies and effects.
   – RCs and ecumenism before Vatican II. Malines, Couturier.
   – Vatican II – relations with Protestants and Orthodox.
   – ARCIC and other meetings since Vatican II.
   – outstanding problems; achievements.

10. The Liturgical Movement in the Twentieth Century
    – early changes in RC Church; Pius X; Pius XII; Mediator Dei.
    – 1928 Prayer Book.
    – Post-war changes in Eucharist; RC and Protestant.
    – Vatican II: Document on the Liturgy; principles.
    – Paul VI: Reformer of the Mass 1970: Anglican Revisions.
    – ARCIC on the Eucharist: Windsor 1970.

11. The church and Economic, Social and Political Issues in the modern western world
    – social encyclicals; principles and effects.

– work of the World Council of Churches and predecessors: COPEC and life and work.
– Vatican II on the church in the modern world.
– particular issues; property; wages; capitalism; socialism; forms of government; industrialisation.
– effectiveness or not of churches' point of view.

12. The attitude of the Churches to the Third World
   – calls for justice; economic problems.
   – church in the modern world: WCC documents.
   – liberation theology; background, attitudes and effectiveness.
   – church and revolution.

13. Church and Nazism, Communism and Fascism
   – church and politics in the nineteenth century.
   – Russian Revolution and Marxism.
   – Italy and Fascism.
   – church and Germany during the Nazi period.

14. Biblical Criticism in the Twentieth Century
   – growth of the German school – work of Bultmann.
   – developments in England and France.
   – what has it achieved?

15. Science and Religion in the Twentieth Century
   – background – issues of authority.
   – evolution today: Teilhard de Chardin; Humani Generis; Hardy.
   – scientific advances and moral theology, in particular with reference to warfare; biological experimentation; medical science.
   – conflict between science and the doctrine of creation?

16. Second Vatican Council
   – causes – forces within the church.
   – what the Council produced.
   – new ideas on the 'church' – tensions and changes.
   – assessment.

17. Anglican Spirituality in the Twentieth Century
   – Evelyn Underhill and Mark Gibbard.

18. The Twentieth Century Monastic Tradition
   – Thomas Merton.
   – Basil Hume.

19. Contemporary Orthodox Spirituality
   – Anthony Bloom.
   – Kallistos Ware.

20. The Charismatic Movement
   – Simon Tugwell.

21. The Spirituality of the Desert in the Twentieth Century
    – Réné Voillaume.
    – Charles de Foucauld.
    – Ruth Burrows.
    – Carlo Coretto.

NOTES

1. James Clark, 'The Great Sacrifice'.
2. Cf. Editorial Comment on the Leamington Spa Syllabus.

6 Theology in the Classroom within the Present Educational Setting: Problems and Prescriptions

Brenda Watson

I have long been of the opinion that all children should be introduced to theology in the classroom, and that it should feature as a major option for advanced study in every school. The chances of either aspiration being fulfilled are, however, still remote in this country. The educational system is not geared towards encouraging theological propensities: indeed it would be more accurate to say that it effectively operates against such a pursuit. I should like therefore first in this paper to draw attention to certain salient disturbing features of the present situation, known doubtless to all but easily overlooked. I shall refer to state schools but much of the analysis impinges, directly or indirectly, upon denominational education. As theology hardly anywhere exists as a subject in its own right, I shall be concerned with religious education, of which it ought to form a significant part.

1. The cinderella-status of religious education

The situation is precarious and presents a number of highly disturbing features. Let a few facts and figures speak for themselves: only fifty-eight per cent of all secondary schools provide religious education for all fourth-formers, twenty-four per cent provide it for some, often for the less academically able only, and eighteen per cent for none at all.[1] Lower down the school a large number allow the subject only one lesson a week or bury it in some integrated general studies. The options system for public examinations also frequently operates against the subject because of the way it is set against subjects the supposed currency-value of which is far greater. In most schools an able pupil would have to be fairly determined to do O or A level Religious Studies. The subject is

frequently discriminated against in other ways, being allowed a very
small capitation allowance, no specialist room and poor promotion
prospects for the unfortunate teacher, who in the worst situations has
to teach to 500 children a week one of the most demanding, controversial
subjects on the timetable. It is hardly surprising that the wastage is
considerable. Well over half the religious education teachers at present
working in state secondary schools are in their first five years of teaching.
Of the more experienced, some become disillusioned because they see
their task as hopeless, others seek status and financial improvement by
accepting posts of responsibility in other areas of the school curriculum,
pastoral work, careers, liberal studies, sixth form studies and so forth.
Except in Roman Catholic schools, a Scale 4 post is rare, and a Scale 3
is also increasingly unlikely. Religious education has been a shortage
area with regard to recruitment for years and a recent DES Secondary
School Staffing Survey[2] showed religious education in the lowest place
with regard to teachers qualified to teach it. It is estimated indeed that
in maintained secondary schools only forty per cent of tuition in religious
education is given by teachers properly qualified for teaching it, and
that twenty-nine per cent is in the hands of people with no qualifications
whatsoever in religious education.[3] A Religious Education adviser
mournfully commented to me recently that unless something drastic
happens there will soon be no religious education teachers of a
competence comparable to that in other areas of the curriculum.

The situation with regard to teacher-training does not immediately
refute such pessimism. Only ten colleges of education which have
survived the cyclone of closure can offer religious studies to secondary
level in their B.Ed. degree courses. Postgraduate training presents a
similar picture: in university departments less than half again offer a
main method course in religious studies and only three colleges and
institutes of higher education do.[4] One encouraging sign is that the
number of students opting for these courses has increased in university
departments from about 138 in 1980 to about 158 in 1981, and in the
rest from about 178 in 1980 to 205 in 1981.[5] This is still a very small
number by comparison with the 9,500 students in training for the
teaching profession. It must also be noted that some of these students
take more than one method-course. Religious studies as a second study
is currently suggested by government officials as being a way round the
difficulty but as a recent HMI discussion paper warns:

> the level of academic and professional knowledge the student has
> achieved in his 'second' subject is crucial. . . the effectiveness (of
> method-work) is governed by the quality of the student's learning in

the subject itself. The specialist needs to have studied, and to continue to study, his subject in sufficient depth to understand the essential processes which operate within it, and this means far more than acquiring a body of knowledge. There is legitimate ground for questioning how far most students are capable of gaining this depth of understanding of more than one subject, or at most of two closely related subjects.[6]

Clearly much must depend upon the re-training of teachers in in-service programmes and here all kinds of factors, financial, and others, act as constraints.

This low status in schools reflects the relative lack of concern for the subject among educationalists. I think it would be fair to say that only a small minority regard religious education as important. Few deny in theory that religious education should feature as a small part in a child's education, but very few will give it breathing-space in practice. Recent government documents bemoan deficiencies in the sciences, modern languages and so forth, but express little concern for or understanding of religious education.[7]

2. *The role of theology within religious education*

Even amongst those who advocate religious education vociferously the case for the inclusion of theology has to be fought. Belief in the fact or desirability of a pluralist society, a strong inclination towards relativism and a vestigial acceptance of certain Christian tenets such as love for one's neighbour and respect for the autonomy of the child, have combined to promote a phenomenological approach in which, if theology is done at all, it is very much at second-hand. In recent years awareness of the inadequacy of this approach, in that it ignores the real needs and questions of young people, has produced the demand for education in values. But once again the *human* dimension is placed at the forefront. Any real engagement with the content of what people believe *for its own sake*, and serious questions as to its truth, are still evaded. The bitter legacy of denominational acidity on doctrinal grounds has taught many sincere educationalists to fear controversy at the level of what is really meaningful to a person, and, as what they would regard as 'assured consensus' is not arrived at by academic theologians, they avoid theology. Where, however, the theological debate is deemed to be appropriate in school this is regarded as only understandable by the very few. In the almost complete absence of early theological teaching, these suspicions are constantly being reinforced! Furthermore, theology normally suffers from a third defect:

it does not comply with the required standard of 'relevance'! Even where its importance is acknowledged, and these hurdles successfully vanquished, there still remains the volume of other material which it is deemed essential to include in religious education. Theology can only claim a small share of precious time and resources.

3. *The inhibiting influence of syllabus and examination structures*

The school syllabus may be regarded as a device to prop up the incompetent and fetter the potentially good teacher. An enormous amount of care and energy is normally expended on its compilation and it not infrequently affords an aesthetic satisfaction to the beholder, replete as it is with all the right aims and objectives, balanced content and interesting variety of methodology. The same is true of the examination syllabuses offered by the various boards. They would appear to furnish some scope for theology, and to require some depth of study whilst ensuring adequate breadth. And yet so often a gulf is fixed between the intention and the performance. The teacher feels constrained to keep to the syllabus without regard to his/her own interests or those of the pupils. Shortage of time and lack of command of the contents to be taught conspire to prevent that freedom and personal involvement which can generate an enquiring and sometimes indeed luminous atmosphere for learning. The uniqueness of each individual and of each class, the members of which have a wide variety of backgrounds, experience and knowledge, constitutes so important an unknown factor that any syllabus *qua* syllabus is likely to be unsuitable.[8] Particularly in an area such as theology, it is important that prejudices, misunderstandings and doubts should be allowed to surface and be properly dealt with. Authentic thinking by pupils requires time and opportunity to develop, and is dependent on a high level of motivation which is jeopardized by adherence to syllabus. And yet extremely detailed syllabus construction continues to be required by many heads of department, headteachers and validating boards such as CNAA.

The examination-system itself is, even at best, a blunt tool for education and at worse its executioner. There is a growing public concern about its limitations in its present form. The HMI discussion paper, *Teacher Training and the Secondary School*, already quoted, begins by deprecating 'the emphasis on factual recall rather than an understanding of underlying ideas and concepts. There is much over-directed teaching, particularly for those pupils who are being entered for examinations beyond their capacity. . .' The Council of Subject Teaching Associations currently urges that the examination system should arise out of the curriculum, not the other way round. They are concerned that 'the activities, teaching strategies and learning styles adopted by Schools tend to be restricted to those which have examinable outcomes'. They advocate 'profile' reporting of pupil performance in examinations, together with the adoption of a wider range of assessment techniques to help 'free the curriculum from the worst effects of examination requirements', and they would like to see examination boards 'reduce significantly the amount of syllabus content'.

The 'Manifesto for Change', published in the *Times Educational Supplement* on 30 January 1981[9] and signed by a very representative selection of public figures in church and state, had this to say:

> The system which herds young people into examination halls every year for a once-for-all race with the clock, upon which their personal status in society depends, is becoming increasingly inappropriate. It distorts the curriculum, excludes vital elements in education, generates a damaging sense of failure among a large section of the student population, and positively rejects – at great risk to society – some 10 to 20% of the 'least able'. It also trains young people in intense academic competitiveness at a time when cooperative skills are everywhere in demand. Furthermore, the system *cannot* be fair.

Perhaps the most serious indictment of the system is that the prestige of examinations causes the non-examinable seven-eighths of the iceberg to be relegated to a second place in the minds of teachers, children, parents and employers. This includes the all-important area of attitudes, value-judgments and personal maturity, upon which the quality of academic work itself depends. This is why the 'distancing' of the candidate from the material under study, which is assumed in almost all A level papers on offer in religious studies, is not helpful: it does little to promote a genuine engagement with the subject, a possible growth in spiritual perception or integration of devotional and scholarly attitudes.

This may seem a gloomy recital, but I fear that it is a realistic appraisal of the situation. Certainly there are many signs of hope: much excellent teaching at every level is being accomplished despite all obstacles, and there are signs of a deeper appreciation amongst many people, including the most influential, of a more balanced approach both to the wider aspects of curriculum and examination work, and to the possibilities of truly religious education. The second part of my paper will discuss the way forward as I see it. But first a few words to the teacher at present in the classroom, on how to salvage something worthwhile under the present system.

1. Suggestions for the individual teacher with regard to A level examination work within the present system

I would strongly advocate encouraging pupils to take responsibility themselves, with the help of notes and selected reading, for covering the basic 'factual' material, (which includes who said what and why X disagrees with Y) in their homework time. One-third of contact time in school could then be allotted to monitoring progress, and training in examination techniques. Present A levels, which require two unseen papers, test, quite apart from content, at least the following skills: performance under stress, ability to choose the right questions, speed of thinking, memory work, style and coherence in expression, and conciseness. It is important therefore to employ such tactics as quick memory tests and other assignments which drill candidates in writing quickly, sometimes on a prepared theme and sometimes on one requiring speedy choice. It is frequently highly beneficial to set pupils to mark each other's essays, commenting and awarding points for accuracy, coherence of structure, conciseness and so forth. This reduces the burden of marking for the teacher who then has time to correct with extreme care and precision one or two essays by each pupil each term. Experience shows that so often faults and difficulties become habitual, whatever the content of the essay, and the remedy lies in really detailed and time-consuming discussion with the pupil in question. The all-important factor is in encouraging pupils to teach themselves. Much progress here should have been made in the lower years of schooling, but often sixth-formers are still extremely naive with regard to finding appropriate information in their reading and having confidence to express it in their own words and to engage in dialogue with it.

The remaining two-thirds of lesson-time can then be spent in exploring wider issues related to the topics, in following up in some depth queries, difficulties, controversial points made by pupils and in developing their powers of articulation, sensitivity and critical acumen. This 'freeing' of the timetable is enormously helpful. It allows for proper motivation to develop and for project work by more independent-minded pupils, and it furnishes opportunities for creating in the microcosm of the classroom a truly academic community in which sharing of ideas matters. The sheer interest and importance and attractiveness of the subject can then surface. In particular, the theological implications inherent in all aspects of official syllabuses, whether biblical, church history, modern questions, ethics, world religions, can be brought out and discussed. If a paper actually centres on theology, clearly the opportunities are greater still.

If it be objected that this two-fold organizational approach would demand too much preparation by the over-worked teacher in order to ensure that the examination work *per se* was satisfactorily covered in half the time normally allowed it, I would reply that such preparations can and should be at the service of the rest of the teaching commitments of the teacher. Work in religious education can resolve itself into certain salient themes which are recurrent and require constant return to them at a deeper level. It follows that if the themes for public examinations are chosen with this in mind they can be appropriate for all ages and be dealt with doubtlessly in different ways. It needs, in any case, to be remembered that no two groups of students are alike, and should not be treated as such. Variety in method and emphasis can go hand in hand with depth of preparation of content.

2. *Contributions to promoting public advocacy of theology in the classroom*

There is much that teachers, lecturers, parents, church laity and clergy can do to stimulate a change in the climate of public opinion.

(*a*) The publicity in the market place as in the Senior Common Room of a rationale for theology which really meets the case of the secularly-minded educationalist. I have already mentioned the three kinds of objections to it which cause people to feel uneasy. The most serious is the charge of indoctrination, and so although this theme is also considered by John Kent[10] I would like to reiterate here that the educational aim is not to convert to a point of view, or to evangelize in the sense of wanting the pupils to accept a certain interpretation of the doctrine; it is rather, to try to convey sufficient understanding of the religious concepts involved to enable the pupils to make their own authentic and intelligent decisions about these concepts.[11] Naturally, any teacher who holds sincere convictions himself will be glad if some of the pupils do come to share those convictions, but – and here is the built-in check against abuse – only if the pupil has freely and genuinely reached that same conclusion. This means in practice that a good teacher would have cause for grave concern if a large number in the class did not disagree with him on a number of points.[12] Complete agreement would be an indication either of basic indifference and non-involvement, for to think deeply involves an element of doubt and questioning which cannot be lightly resolved, or of lack of freedom which could be due to authoritarian attitudes or to the sheer persuasiveness of a mature mind which easily overawes the immature. The good teacher will therefore seek to jerk the pupils into thought, not to present a ready-made opinion on a plate. The controversial nature of theology renders it an excellent topic for stimulating thought, and this is the opposite of indoctrination, of inducing mental inertia.

I would make one addendum. John Macquarrie, in a recent paper entitled 'Why Theology?' argued that theology requires, besides reflection upon, participation *in* the religious *faith* thus brought to conscious verbal expression.[13] I submit that theological reflection can be engaged in without even the minimal commitment he suggests. Study should be such as to enable the possibility of such intelligent participation to occur. It is necessary to make such a distinction because otherwise the educational justification for wishing *all* pupils to receive some theological grounding is defective. Such participation in faith cannot be assumed on the part of all pupils or students, even in those who opt for the subject, and such an assumption would raise the charge of indoctrination. The importance of participation relates to what may be termed *significant* theology. Its nature is such that awareness of the need for such participation is a sign of a mature grasp of the subject. The analogy with music is close: musicianship is not an initial qualification for entering upon its study, but becomes realized as more and more essential as the inherent structure of music is perceived, and if any serious original contribution to it is to be made.

The charge of the difficulty of theology is one which affects A level work indirectly, in that although most educationalists would concede that able pupils of 16+ can appreciate its complex concepts, younger children experience problems and therefore they should be shielded from the rigours of theology: consequently much work of a remedial nature has to be undertaken in the sixth forms. The case for promoting the theological thinking of even infants needs to be put forward. Difficulties should be seen as stimulating the professional capacities of the teacher to rise to the occasion and devise ways of helping children to understand. A serious listening to children's questions, a variety of teaching techniques, the willingness to develop topics in depth and, above all, the teacher's own continuing wrestling with theological problems and refusal to take refuge in theological jargon, can all contribute to overcoming this obstacle.

The charge of irrelevance arises from preoccupation with utilitarian and with human-centred concerns on the part of adults, and of the assumption that this is so for pupils also. Attempts, laudable in themselves, to discuss immediate natural interests and ethical matters, whether in primary or secondary religious education, frequently do not arrive at theology at all, because having once started in the human, secular situation there appears to be no logical reason whatever for introducing talk about God. Theology has to be consciously and openly introduced.

The utilitarian objection can be answered in at least two ways: firstly it disregards the place of sheer interest and desire to understand and appreciate, which is just as valid and may be less self-centred an impulse behind the discipline of learning. In the teaching of English, for example, the criterion for a topic's inclusion is by no means always that it is seen to be relevant, therefore why must this be so in religious education? The intensity of interest which teenagers show when they are allowed to discuss religious matters freely, suggests that there is a strong desire to understand more of this strange language-game. Various surveys reinforce this general impression that most adolescents have a basically positive though doubting approach, and that not infrequently they feel 'let down' by superficial teaching. Surveys by even 'progressive' educationalists have suggested this to be so for the past two decades. Secondly, the apparent divorce between beliefs and actual life situations, between orthopraxis and orthodoxy, must be exposed for the fallacy it is. As John Macquarrie argued in the paper already referred to, 'belief and action really go together. They interact with one another.'[14]

(*b*) I have spent some time on this consideration of the rationale for theology because of its importance. Related to it is the need to dispel the anxieties felt by many religious people that academic theology has a dangerous effect on faith. Theologians must be aware of their responsibility to society – much theology has been exceedingly negative, and has encouraged severe scepticism and uncertainty; the public array of private doubts is dangerous, because so often the affirmations which sustain the critical conclusions are not recognized or shared. Academic theology should always seek to be creative, helping people to build up their aspirations and beliefs. I have previously spelt out some of the factors which govern such creative disputation, and which can enable it to be the servant of spirituality,[15] a theme developed by Father Timothy Wright in Chapter 4.

(*c*) There needs to be a campaign to seek to make examinations more positive in encouragement of such an approach. This would involve, I submit, a change of focus in the type of questions set, and a wider range of assessment techniques. The whole structure of the examination system is under debate at the moment and will continue to be so in the next few years. The time is ripe for the airing of views and possibly even radical changes. The Joint Council of GCE and CSE Boards for 16+ National Criteria has gathered opinions with regard to the educational aims, assessment objectives, content, and techniques of assessment with suggestions for weighting and grading. It is at present drawing up

Brenda Watson

a report. Submissions to the Parliamentary Select Committee on Education, Science and the Arts have been sent in by organizations such as COSTA, the Religious Education Council, and the Association for Religious Education in respect of its inquiry into 'Secondary Education and Examinations'. The Department of Education and Science is concerned with the possible introduction of an Intermediate Level Examination taken at 18+ which will require half the time over two years of present A level courses. Its purpose would be in broadening the studies undertaken by some of those who currently successfully take full A level courses. Such an examination may well encourage some of the more able sixth formers to opt for religious studies or theology. It is important therefore that people's views are expressed at this time of re-thinking.

I have previously expressed views on the type of questions which can encourage authentic thinking and on the values of 'seen' examinations.[16] I would argue that if the latter is balanced by an 'unseen' examination and with project work such as that which at present, many Boards offer at O and CSE levels, together with oral assessment as appropriate, a deeper engagement with theology would be encouraged. I append to this paper a summary I prepared for a meeting with AEB in 1979 arguing the case for the 'seen' examination element in assessment. I would suggest a weighting of thirty-three per cent for each of the three essential component parts of the examination: 'unseen', 'seen' and project.

3. Implications for the training of teachers

In an organized educational setting, the calibre of the teacher is the most significant single factor. The baneful or beneficial effects of his/her character and attitude are quickly apparent, and pupils learn most effectively what is exemplified not what is stated. The substitution of very fair, indeed often impeccable, aims and objectives for practice does not deceive even the slow learner who experiences the impact of the teacher's personality. The HMI discussion paper on teacher training, already referred to, criticizes the predominantly passive role into which so many pupils are forced in school, but comments that often the college experience of teachers reinforces such an approach:

> Many course programmes depend heavily on the set lecture, with the ensuing tutorial almost equally dominated by the tutor. However sound the precepts expressed on the matter of teaching methodology, the example offered sometimes presents students with models remarkably similar to those criticized as prevalent in schools. Much of what is said about note-taking, passive listening, and restricted

reading applies with equal force to the experience of many students. Practice of this kind transmits to them a clear message about the roles of teacher and learner.[17]

Yet as the paper points out, 'the quality of learning is more important than the quantity'. It goes on to advocate 'more small group work which genuinely involves student participation'.[18]

I agree that such a step is in the right direction. The compulsory lecture should be a rare inspirational occasion, and the seminar groupings small enough to permit even the most reticent to have the courage to speak. Proper motivation is encouraged if students may study different topics. Reading should be for the purpose of promoting a quality of reflective-ness which is supremely important for theology. Such an unstructured non-uniform approach requires courage, even though it is a logical development from the kind of educational philosophy accepted as almost axiomatic. If this were actually experienced in college, more teachers might have the courage to introduce it into schools where such a less structured approach could, for example, enable individuals to study much more on their own under directional help, relieve the burden of establishing a just options-system, satisfy the need for individual choice and promote cross-fertilization of subjects. The latter is an important consideration. The integrity of subjects must be maintained but compartmentalism is as inimical to producing good academic standards as it is to educational aims. Students need to be encouraged to see things as a whole, and to be concerned not only with education *in* a subject but also with education *through* a subject. Many colleges have experimented, with greater or less success, with foundation courses designed to help students towards an harmonious understanding of separate areas of study. Such courses often get staff into dialogue who before were strangers to each other's works. Often too they reveal extreme vagueness with regard to the specific concepts, skills and modes of evidence of the different disciplines. It can be salutary for a religious education lecturer to realize how much of his syllabus is historical, sociological or philosophical, and how infrequently it contains anything distinctive at all. The confusion of the staff spills over into the way the students receive the course, especially because in the midst of the plethora of new courses being drawn up each year in almost all establishments of higher education, lack of confidence is compensated for in mounds of verbiose paper-work. A foundation course in which I was myself required to take part was literally drowned in an ocean of words, and vastly over-structured. In the end, the best way to train teachers of theology is to encourage them to *become* theologians.[19]

In bringing yet one more ocean of words to a conclusion I would like to end on an optimistic note. We live in exciting times. In a sense, I believe we are approaching a watershed as regards the educational scene. A remarkable pioneer experiment to educate *every* child has been operating now sufficiently long for its many defects, deficiencies and limitations to be more clearly apparent, not just to the few farseeing idealists, but increasingly to the general public. Yet economic recessions and rival political machinations, together with great ignorance or a sense of helplessness in view of the size of the problem, are also at work. It is the privilege and responsibility of all of us who care about the education of the young to do what we can to ensure that future changes promote a genuinely religious and theological education for all.

APPENDIX

The Value of 'Seen' Examinations

I should like to promote discussion on a particular type of assessment which has so far not found its way into public examinations although used occasionally in schools and colleges, namely, a paper which is sat under normal examination conditions (of silence, timing, and strict scrutiny of any papers and/or books brought into the examination room) but the questions on which have been seen by the candidate at least two terms before the examination date.

When on the staff of a college of education I had the opportunity of experimenting in such a method of examining. I was compelled to conclude that the results were very favourable in encouraging high motivation and depth of thinking on the part of students. I found they responded well to the need to stay with a theme long enough to be aware of its ramifications, and to formulate their own opinions which they could back up with evidence. It helped to release their study from pre-occupation with memorizing a large amount of so-called 'factual' material, much of which tended to be at a very superficial level involving the use of ill-understood jargon, name-dropping and a general non-involvement with the subject. It was liberating also for lecturers because instead of feeling constrained to offer a wide coverage of questions so that candidates would be able to tackle the unknown paper, it allowed themes to be developed according to their instrinsic interest and importance and relevance to the students concerned. Such an approach encourages what would seem to be the proper purpose of education: genuine engagement with learning, the chief motive for which is interest, and awareness of the value of what is studied. Such an endeavour normally requires work in *depth* and with a degree of *flexibility*, to promote the essential voluntary element. Furthermore, I found that the 'seen' examination largely overcame one of the greatest disadvantages of the examination system, namely that what is being assessed is nervous disposition. It is openly acknowledged that large numbers of candidates are adversely affected by the conditions of stress which the 'now-or-never' atmosphere of the examination causes and that therefore examinations are a blunt tool for assessing ability and understanding of a subject. It is not possible to equate academic excellence with a calm and unruffled temperament. Anything which can mitigate this problem is to be welcomed, and to take away the element of surprise is certainly one such consideration.

I was convinced therefore by this experience that a 'seen' examination paper provided the best opportunity for fulfilling what would seem to be the basic aims of an examination: (*a*) to provide a reliable guide to academic ability and standard of work achieved; (*b*) to promote good teaching in the classroom or lecture-room.

There are a number of points I would like to clarify before giving some examples for consideration.

1. It would be important to give the paper at least two terms before the examination date, otherwise the educational value of the scheme is largely lost. An unholy raid upon the library, frantic cribbing and rushed preparation could increase anxiety and a mark-grabbing attitude. The success of the 'seen' examination depends on its allowing time to candidates to produce something authentic and well understood.

2. It is clearly important that the questions posed on the paper are stimulating and thought-provoking, and that it is made clear to candidates that a high proportion of marks will be awarded on the quality of thinking expressed. The holding of opinions should be encouraged provided that the candidate can put forward evidence in support. It must be insisted that the candidate will be penalized not for holding an opinion with which the examiner happens to disagree but only for the superficiality or absence of reasons given for the opinion. The assessment of what qualifies as suitable reasons must depend on the subject-matter in question, just as it does in the marking of unseen papers. Candidates would in a similar way be expected to show evidence of appropriate reading and consideration of the nature of the subject.

3. The nature of 'religious studies' requires that the controversial aspect of beliefs, values and practices be taken seriously. Straightforward apparently 'factual' material is only at the periphery, and serious damage can be done to any genuine understanding of religion unless

questions of interpretation, the difficulty of establishing generalizations, the relationship between beliefs, and practice and so on, are exposed. Awareness of such issues *is* the proper concern of secondary school religious education at whatever level of ability. Even simple questions can and should have this dimension. This type of examination paper is therefore as appropriate for the less academically able as for the more able.

4. It would be important that the questions posed on the 'seen' paper are of a fundamental nature in that for their answering they require a firm grasp of the nature of the subject as a whole, and considerable breadth of knowledge at the appropriate level. This would effectively counter the objection that unscrupulous teachers or candidates would concentrate on a much smaller area than the time allotted to study warrants. In view of the common fault, especially apparent in religious studies, of attempting breadth of content without permitting depth of understanding, one of the chief values of the 'seen' examination would be precisely in narrowing content area. Insistence on the development of appropriate skills and of awareness of the inter-relationship between different areas of religious studies which occurs when the ramifications of a given theme are developed in religious studies should ensure that acknowledgment at least is made of the many other areas of which one is ignorant. Realism as regards content is essential for any sense of achievement by teacher or candidates, but equally awareness of the vastness and complexity of the subject is called for, and is possible with the less academically able as well as with the able.

5. Examination conditions for the actual writing of answers will ensure that they are the candidate's own work. If notes are allowed into the examination room, these should be forfeit after the examination is over, and the candidate given to understand that such notes should only contain appropriate quotations with acknowledgment of their source which can be checked or an outline plan containing only odd words or short phrases.

6. It is worth noting that there is less likelihood of 'cribbed' answers and second-hand thinking in a 'seen' examination than in an 'unseen', because questions which require some depth of thinking would be expected to produce very varying answers. Any close comparison would be immediately suspect. This could and should be pointed out to candidates.

7. I would advocate that the option of an oral examination at the examiner's discretion should be included so that cases where collusion is suspected, or where a clever 'memorized' answer is suggested, can be investigated, and the candidate required to develop or explicate in

a different way the statements he has written. Although it is desirable on other grounds to make the oral examination an integral part of the assessment itself, because of the constraints of time and money it would probably be wise to regard the oral component as simply a deterrent against abuse of the freedom given in the 'seen' examination.

8. Skills of verbalization and the ability to use concepts central to religion are essential for any understanding of religion which is examinable at sixteen plus. This does *not* mean that such an examination is a test in English language. Small vocabulary, poor grammar, bad spelling, inadequate punctuation, lack of style, should *not* be penalized provided that the candidate can communicate what he intends. (Cf. a candidate is not penalized for his hand-writing, providing it is legible).

9. The 'seen' examination could be adequate as the sole method of assessment, provided the safeguard of an oral examination was built-in. This would allow for simplicity of structure and economy in effort of examining. But it could equally form part, and I would advocate not less than thirty-three per cent, of a combined method of assessment; the other parts could include a project and/or an unseen test of certain very clearly defined basic skills.

To conclude, the advantages of the 'seen' examination would seem to be as follows:

1. Minimization of anxiety and fear on the part of candidates;
2. the opportunity to set more challenging questions, and to require a higher standard of answer;
3. The likelihood of a wider spread of marks;
4. Encouragement of genuine critical involvement with the subject-matter by the candidate which for the subject of 'religious studies' is essential;
5. Offering, therefore, a more reliable method of assessment of ability and standard of work reached;
6. Stimulating authentic thinking in depth which is fostering the proper ends of education and encouraging teachers to concentrate on educating their students rather than on preparing candidates as such.

In the present situation, where so many are dissatisfied with what is happening in religious education and are concerned about raising standards, fighting ignorance, apathy and prejudice, and securing for it the proper consideration on educational grounds which in any comprehensive, liberal system of education it deserves, examinations of the above type could play a quite crucial role.

Note

It may be helpful if I articulate some of the principles which form the educational thinking behind my advocacy of the 'seen' examination:

1. 'Factual' statements as in other subjects like history need to be justified. The straightforward 'facts' in religion are in fact generalizations or interpretations, or partake of the nature of historical 'facts' as being based on evidence regarded as virtually irrefutable by the majority of scholars. Even candidates of less ability should and can be aware of this. Thus the work required of them can be scholarly, though relatively simple. Standards of attempted accuracy and awareness of the difficulty of arriving at true statements can be developed at *all* levels of ability.

2. Purely cerebral understanding is at the level of second-hand thinking and contributes very little, if anything, to genuine understanding, which in all subjects, and especially in religion, involves what may be termed the affective or the intuitive. Examinations ought to encourage and acknowledge this aspect of understanding despite the difficulties of drawing up a marking-scheme. 'Involvement' with the subject tends not to be called for, and is often discouraged, by 'unseen' examinations.

3. Religion is controversial at its very roots, therefore if indoctrination is to be avoided on the one hand, and a watering-down which fails to give pupils any adequate awareness of religion on the other hand, it is essential to enable candidates to enjoy, and to explore, the vital issues of interpretation and opinion, together with the possibility of serious commitment on their part. To fail to provide an arena for such responsible thinking cannot be termed educational. Examinations could play a crucial role precisely in providing the element of discipline beneficial for such discussion and reflection.

NOTES

1. *Aspects of Secondary Education in England*, HMSO 1979, p. 23, Table H.

2. Findings available in DES document, *Statistical Bulletin*, 5/82.

3. Parliamentary reply by Dr Rhodes Boyson, March 1982, quoted in *Religious Education Directory* ed. Brian E. Gates, Religious Education Council of England and Wales, p. 143.

4. Figures confirmed by telephone conversation with DES, 1 June 1983.

5. See *Religious Education Directory*, pp. 154f.

6. *Teacher Training and the Secondary School*, The Implications of the HMI National Secondary Survey, HMI Discussion Paper, DES 1981, pp. 7f.

7. Eg., *Framework for the Curriculum*, 1980; *Examinations 16–18*, 1980; *P.G.C.E. in the Public Sector*, 1980, pp. 2f.; and *Teaching Quality*, 1983, pp. 10, 26.

8. See chapter 4, p. 70.

9. Quoted in the House of Commons Report for the Education, Science and Arts Committee 1981–2 on *The Secondary School Curriculum and Examinations*, p. xxxi.

10. See chapter 7, pp. 109f.

11. See chapter 4, p. 72 (Jamison).

12. See chapter 3, p. 55.

13. John Macquarrie, 'Why Theology', given at the Farmington Conference held at Keble College, Oxford, 2–6 January 1979, and published in the Conference Report, *Religious Studies and Public Examinations* ed. E. Hulmes and B. Watson, 1980, pp. 35f.

14. Ibid., p. 35.

15. Watson, 'Examinations in Religious Studies: Preparation in Education for an Awareness of the Spiritual' in *Religious Studies and Public Examinations*, pp. 22–5.

16. Ibid., pp. 29–33.

17. *Teacher Training and the Secondary School*, pp. 11f.

18. Ibid., p. 12.

19. See chapter 9, p. 138.

7 The Modern Masters and Religious Education

John Kent

An important change of emphasis in the teaching of religion in schools seems to have occurred in the later 1960s. It may be connected with the publication of Professor Ninian Smart's book, *Secular Education and the Logic of Religion*, in which he criticized attempts to 'arouse faith in school-children', but suggested that the aim of religious education should be to establish their capacity to understand religious pheno-mena.[1] Professor Smart's own language was ambiguous, and at times his book was actually used to defend 'arousing faith'. As for understanding religious phenomena, it has been argued that most children need to be at least fourteen years of age before they can stand back and look at religion as though it were a subject for study.[2] And if one accepts this argument, as I do myself, it follows that the present balance of religious education in schools is highly unsatisfactory, because 'understanding religious phenomena' is a course for the sixth form, a stage in the progress of a child who gets that far when he or she is not likely to be taking an A level in the subject. One has also to grant, of course, that as things stand sixth-formers lose little by not taking such an A level, because so much of what is generally taught revolves around worn-out attitudes to the text of the Old and New Testaments. Moreover, the 'Agreed Syllabuses' have failed to agree on either the syllabus or the aims of religious education: 'many secondary teachers ended up with a syllabus which amalgamated three different approaches to the subject'.[3] Such material was unlikely to do much either to arouse faith or to help towards an understanding of religious phenomena, though one guesses that in practice the former is more likely than the latter. The value of such faith or understanding is limited; we constantly expect people to derive from educational experiences offered them when they are young what they will only come to realize, if they realize it at all, later in life at greater cost. The value of religious education is that *adults* should have more than just a simple, secular frame of reference for interpreting life when it finally overwhelms them, something more than our contemporary secular culture which now dabbles as easily in the occult as it previously rejected 'God'.[4]

Nevertheless, these A levels in religious subjects largely reflect the past belief of many Christians that through revelation Christianity possesses divinely-given, unique knowledge which can be taught in schools as objective fact which ought to be believed. The Trinity, the Incarnation, the Atonement, the Resurrection, the Ascension, and the supernatural character of the church are all frequently referred to as *facts* in popular preaching and contemporary theology. Thus Helmut Thielicke, for example, dismissed doubts about the resurrection of Jesus by making a sophisticated criticism of those who experience the doubts:

> If and so long as we are still in our sins, not having died to sins but being still their captive, we cannot grasp or accept the news of the resurrection. For our concern is still to remain autonomous. We do not want Christ to have power over us. . . Hence the news that Christ is Lord in virtue of his resurrection is unacceptable to us. This is why Wingren can say that in the facticity at issue here is enclosed the facticity of our captivity. Noetically, this captivity takes the form of prejudice.[5]

This sort of revised fundamentalism, when applied to education, requires that religious instruction aim at conversion, or 'arousing faith', because only the regenerate can understand and accept the truths of Christianity. A more complicated example may be found in Karl Rahner's study of the evolution of man as a theological problem.[6] Discussing the relationship between dogma and science, Rahner said that the church's pronouncements contained fundamentally nothing more than a repetition of the biblical accounts:

> It follows that *we do not know* the visible and tangible, concrete details of proto-history (Paradise, Fall). The features of the biblical account which might give the impression of supplying such details, in reality belong to the form of statement, not to what is affirmed. Consequently *we know nothing except that* man was created by God as God's personal partner in a sacred history of salvation and perdition; that concupiscence and death do not belong to man as God wills him to be, but to man as sinner; that the first man was also the

first to incur guilt before God and his guilt as a factor of man's existence *historically* brought about by man, belongs intrinsically to the situation in which the whole subsequent history of humanity unfolds. How all this happened, however, *we do not know*. The question, therefore, how the occurrence of this biblical proto-history fits into the conceptions of the beginnings of mankind entertained by natural science, cannot be precisely formulated at all, because *we do not know* what the occurrence was like in its externals.[7]

Of course, Rahner deserves the credit for aiming at an open solution as far as he can. There remains, nevertheless, the implication that in turning to the sixth-form course in religious education one will assume certain Christian 'facts' as fundamental, as knowledge which can be taught and which ought to be learned. There is no need here to 'arouse faith' necessarily, but the question is bound to be asked: what would one be asking children to understand as 'religious phenomena' – a specifically Christian dogmatic theology, presented as true because revealed; or – and this is much more likely to stir up problems – the role of myth in late twentieth-century Christianity? One can hardly expect to be allowed to teach a systematic theology as true (fact) outside the borders of a specific religious community which provides the theological system with a supporting and confirming sub-culture. Outside the religious sub-culture, that is, and not least in the state-school system, a systematic theology, whether Christian or non-Christian, will be regarded by many pupils as no more than a bundle of hypotheses, though this may be countered to some extent by insisting on the difference between a purely dogmatic approach to religious education, and a historical approach which would show how this bundle of Christian hypotheses had played a vital role in the development of Western culture as a whole, as well as in the interpretation and fostering of man's religious life. The churches still obscure the issue, however, to the extent that they cling to their traditional hegemony over religious education in the state-school system, and it is this which gives continuing importance to what I have called 'revised fundamentalism'.[8]

The assertion that religious education is bound to aim at the 'arousing of faith' might be supported, however, by an appeal to the meditations of the philosopher, Ludwig Wittgenstein:

It strikes me that a religious belief could only be something like a passionate commitment (leidenschaftliche sichentscheiden) to a system of reference. Hence, although it is *belief*, it is really a way of living, or a way of assessing life. It is passionately seizing hold of (leidenschaftliches Ergreifen) this interpretation. Instruction in a religious faith, therefore, would have to take the form of a portrayal, a description, of that system of reference, while at the same time being an appeal to conscience (ein in's Gewissen reden). And this combination would have to result in the pupil himself of his own accord passionately taking hold of the system of reference. It would be as though someone were first to let me see the hopelessness of my situation and then show me the means of rescue until, of my own accord, or not at any rate led by my *instructor*, I ran to it and grasped it.[9]

There is a simple ambiguity here, in as much as although Wittgenstein's instructor must be aiming at conversion, only the pupil can validly change his way of living for himself and take on a new assessment of life. And it is the pupil's behaviour which the instructor has to try to change by describing a new interpretation of existence which will suddenly, if the approach works, lock into what Wittgenstein called the pupil's conscience and revolutionize his stance.

As a model for classroom teaching this sounds plausible even to someone in the radical Protestant tradition, or at least it does so until one turns one's mind back to recent historical experience, to the seductive political totalitarianism of the twentieth century which so often made the classroom the scene of concentrated, persuasive, subtly indirect assaults on the untoughened, vulnerable consciences of the young. Anyone who has visited East European cities like Prague and kept his eyes open suddenly realizes that the absence of God is as nothing to the absence of critical books and newspapers which might educate the mind to resist the kind of conversion which the regime favours. The history of European culture could be written in terms of a constant shifting between dogma, censorship and toleration. Religious groups in the schools and universities of democratic societies have sometimes shown a similar aggression against the personality – in Protestant fundamentalism, for example, and in sectarian anti-intellectualism (the Moonies, for example). Wittgenstein's summary of religious development sounds attractive: portrayal of the system of reference, an appeal to conscience – but however passionate the consequent grasp of the system, however 'authentic' the personal surrender, no political or religious system of reference should be spared a colder, less self-absorbed examination than he implies, one which is not concerned with pictures and signs of sincerity, but asks how the subtle shift has been accomplished which seems to have assimilated religious beliefs to factual beliefs, and even given the resurrection of Christ, for example, more than the status of myth.

Wittgenstein himself, of course, specifically rejected the Christian 'system'. When he isolated the problem of assent as it applied to himself he wrote, in 1937:

> I read that 'No man can say that Jesus is the Lord, but by the Holy Ghost'. And it is true: I cannot call him *Lord*, because that says nothing to me. I could call him 'the paragon', even 'God' – or rather, I can understand it when he is so called; but I cannot utter the word 'Lord' with meaning. *Because I do not believe* that he will come to judge me; because that says nothing to me. And it could say something to me only if I lived *completely* differently.[10]

The Christian idea of the lordship of Jesus, that is, offered him no intelligible or useful grounds of assent; the picture of Christ's return in judgment simply called out no response. And in such a case what one would require, Wittgenstein suggested, before one could believe in ideas like that of the Return in Judgment, would be an overall image of a religious system of reference (in effect an explanatory system) which made at the same time an effective appeal to conscience, so that one glimpsed a totally different way of living, in which it made sense and therefore became possible to assent to the lordship of Jesus and the picture of his return in judgment. This does not mean that Wittgenstein thought that in any foreseeable future he could be convinced in this way that Christ would return to judge him; there should always be grounds for assent beyond the appeal to authority. Outside the classroom, however, and away from the difficulties raised by the specifically Christian New Testament narratives and the theological systems developed from them in the Pauline and other theoretical parts of the primitive documents of the faith, Wittgenstein thought that the process he had envisaged might work out successfully without doing violence either to conscience or to the mind's need to be given adequate grounds for belief or to the personality's insistence on its own integrity. He said, for example, in 1950, that life could educate men to a belief in God, not through visions and other forms of experience which purported to convey the divine existence, but through sufferings of various kinds. Life, that is, could force the concept on us.[11]

The last of these remarks seems to me to go to the root of the problem of religious education. When we talk about 'arousing faith' in children, or of helping them to understand 'religious phenomena', we seem to be assuming that they are able to learn from what is 'taught' in the classroom when they are young, what they will grasp existentially, if indeed they ever grasp it in this sense at all, only later in life. It is one thing if life forces the concept of 'God' upon us,[12] quite another if the enforcement is supposed to be lurking somewhere in the curriculum. At this stage of the discussion, Professor Smart's criticism of any classroom campaign to 'arouse faith' in schoolchildren may be accepted; what remains much less self-evident is that a case can be made for establishing their capacity to understand religious phenomena.

At this point it may prove useful to distinguish even more firmly than before between children from the Christian sub-culture, on the one hand, and children from other, non-Christian sub-cultures on the other. The latter, to the extent that they hear any Christian language at all, hear it as coming to them from an alien source, and this is true even if it reaches them when they attend a state school. These non-Christian children come from the dominant and well-nigh all-pervading culture of our society, a culture of entertainment rather than of ideas. These children are not inherently non-religious, but they prefer religious patterns which pay little attention to traditional, if largely discredited, Christian concepts like 'providence'; they attach more significance to a concept like 'chance', which is just as traditional as the basis of an interpretation of existence, and which seems to them more rational as the ground of behaviour. In the same way, they pay little attention to 'salvation', a Christian concept which has completely lost its grip on popular culture; they attach more value to passage-rites,[13] however enfeebled these have become in the present century, because passage-rites at least make possible the imposition of a temporal order on human experience, and this acts as a reassuring substitute for any more rational, if hypothetical, understanding of existence. The image of a 'divine order', especially if it is described in terms of such Christian concepts as fall-redemption-final judgment, seems unconvincing to the secular, or nearly secular sub-cultures by comparison with ideas of chance and time. Indeed, to many people today chance and time (as maturation and decay) seem self-evident ideas, whereas ideas of a future life or of divine guidance in the present one seem unreal. And it is a hundred years and more since the Journeyman Engineer, Thomas Wright, said that 'if a workingman does not attend a place of worship from an active feeling of religion, he need not do so from any reasons of caste; it is not essential to his maintenance of a character of respectability.'[14] I have written elsewhere of the way in which the nineteenth-century working-class pulled away from the various forms of church-centred respectability and substituted its own pattern of decency, entertainment, and a moderate hope that the universe might turn out to have been trustworthy after all.[15] Little has changed since, except that entertainment has proved the most enduring, because the most vulnerable to commercialism, of the older habits, while hope, however modest, has proved less and less trustworthy. Even when I was writing this (in March 1981), *The Guardian* newspaper carried a sad picture of a small crowd of people praying on a hillside, allegedly for the 'salvation' of a South Wales steelworks. Such events have their own rationale, and in times of economic crisis such invocations of the power of the god take their place within the structure of a universe of chance; but what they illustrate for the mass of the unemployed is the apparent powerlessness of the Christian sub-culture in the temporal order. Chance appears a more rational power on which to stake one's future than a divine order which asserts its willingness to 'care'.

In fact, religious educators, whether in schools or in universities, have to face the fact that British society now includes a non-working class of at least three million, for whom industry will either become a memory or an environment which they will never expect to know. Such a catastrophe can only widen the gulf between what survives of an older middle-class pietism with a variety of denominational allegiances, and what remains of Victorian working-class idealism. In the recent past both Christian education and overseas Christian missions were accustomed to expand in areas where a non-Christian religious tradition was breaking down under the pressure of Western secular and commercial forces – as in Africa, for example, in the late nineteenth and early twentieth centuries. In Britain, however, the working-classes do not seem to be discarding their attachment to their familiar explanatory view of life which relies on such concepts as time and chance. Industrial decline, unpredictable bankruptcies and chronic unemployment have not obviously freed space in which dogmatic religious education can flourish; indeed, the morally indifferent atmosphere of economic depression often seems to reinforce customary disbelief in the value of any kind of education at all. Protestant fundamentalism is essentially a house-wine, marketable only in limited sectors of the religious sub-culture; occultism, faith-healing and exorcism do not perhaps offer the most favourable grounds on which to build an understanding of religious phenomena.

This leads me back to the original problem of the nature and content of religious education. From a purely theological point of view, what is at stake in the conflict between Christian education and popular culture at the level of education is not the plausibility of the total Christian dogmatic system, as far as there is any agreement about such a system's outline. The dogmatic system barely enters the field of discourse. What is at issue in this encounter, which I suppose takes its decisive form at the sixth-form stage in a school, is the prior plausibility of the broader concepts of God, of divine intervention in some form in human life, and of the rationality of human life as we know it in the late twentieth century, where 'rationality' can be glossed in the wildest Hegelian terms or thought of in the plainest common sense. It is evident that a theologian, whether he is a radical Protestant or a Thomist, should not try to tell teachers how to teach. Nevertheless, the theologian can isolate his own kind of problem and give it the kind of treatment which he considers appropriate. Perhaps the major problem here is that a strictly 'Christian education programme' remains a serious possibility only in some corners of the Christian religious sub-culture, in some independent schools, for example. If the wider project, 'religious education', is to survive and to lead back to a renewal of 'Christian education', it will need to restore resonance to a theological vocabulary, to teach sympathetically the religious uses of language, which will almost certainly be forgotten for the time being by the adolescent, but which he or she may recall with existential force when he or she becomes middle-aged. In our present society the teaching of foreign languages in British schools is rapidly collapsing because people do not want to learn Spanish or Italian or German, let alone Russian, when they are young, although they seem quite prepared to do so on their own terms when they are older. Legislation cannot indefinitely protect a subject like religious education, itself the custodian of a language whose uses are not easy to establish, once the mainstream culture doubts their value. One can only draw people's attention back to the possibility that what are now neglected areas of human experience may have permanent significance. Here once more, Wittgenstein's meditations may point a way:

> Christianity is not a doctrine; not, I mean, a theory about what has happened and will happen to the human soul, but a description of something which actually takes place in human life. For 'conscience of sin' is a real event and so are despair and salvation through faith. Those who speak of such things – Bunyan for example, are simply describing what has happened to them, whatever gloss anyone may want to put on it.[16]

For the Christian humanist tradition within which I write, surely the argument about religious education may begin here – I do not mean that it may not begin here for others as well. It starts with the guess, rather than the certainty, that when Bunyan wrote down what had happened to him, he was not just recording in an ideologically conditioned language the kind of psychological suffering and deliverance which can be presented as a by-product of the new, 'modernizing', seventeenth-century market-economy as it impinged on the Puritan

consciousness and theological vocabulary.[17] Of course, one may make
the kind of qualification about *Pilgrim's Progress* which was made by
Wittgenstein, that Bunyan's own interpretation of what had, indubit-
ably, happened to him, could be totally destroyed by insisting on the
ambiguity of his metaphorical system, by saying that all the traps,
quicksands and wrong-turnings of the pilgrimage were planned by the
Lord of the Road, and that he created the monsters and thieves.[18]
Bunyan himself said nothing of the kind, but equally, to suggest this
interpretation of *his* interpretation robbed the latter of its power.
Nevertheless, the force of 'what has happened' remains as a starting-
point, giving one the sense that whatever here may have gone completely
awry, however much the use of a puritan Christian language may have
falsified the analysis of what took place in Bunyan, here at the same
time was one of those fine layers of human experience which remain
part of the common stock, the deposit of hope, which we go on trying
to understand, and which helps to give vitality to the constantly
endangered theological vocabulary. F. R. Leavis put the same conclusion in a different way:

> Bunyan's theological *statement* of the significance he wishes to enforce
> is abstract; but the sense of significance that actually possessed him
> couldn't be stated, it could only be communicated by created means.
> It might be objected that Bunyan identifies the significance of life
> with a belief in a real life that is to come after death, and that therefore
> *Pilgrim's Progress* cannot, for readers who do not share that belief,
> have the kind of virtue that I have attributed to it. But these things
> are not as simple as that. However naively Bunyan, as pastor, might
> have talked of the eternal life as the reward that comes after death
> to the Christian who has persevered through the pains and trials of
> his earthly pilgrimage, the sense of the eternal conveyed by *Pilgrim's
> Progress* and coming from the whole man ('trust the tale', as Lawrence
> said, not the writer) is no mere matter of a life going on and on for
> ever that starts at death. It is a sense of a dimension felt in the earthly
> life – in what for us *is* life, making this something that transcends the
> time succession, transience and evanescence and gives significance.[19]

Christianity is not a doctrine, Wittgenstein said; Bunyan's *theological*
statement of the significance which he wants to convey is abstract,
Leavis said: what matters is the event that lies behind the language, the
kind of event which leaves the man or woman who has experienced it
with a passionate conviction that they do not belong only to themselves.
Not that I imagine that one can hope to convey this sense of human
significance and insignificance, which is the root of religion, by making

modern sixth-formers read *Pilgrim's Progress* for home-work. Theologically, however, there is nowhere else to go – the 'modern masters' may strip religion of its structure and throw us back on the disclosed event, the vague yet powerful impression that only in loss, suffering, and mistrust of all the uses of words can an all-too-human salvation find us out, or find its way out through us – but these are only *their* negations, as powerful in their day as the negations of Calvinism were for Bunyan. Religious educators may start with the 'modern masters', but they are not obliged to end with the conclusion that because the Bible has lost its supernatural authority, the theologian had better give place to the novelist.

Indeed, to reach that conclusion would be to run counter to much recent literary criticism. Gabriel Josipovici, for example, having discovered in the works of authors such as Kafka, Eliot, Stevens and Proust principles which he labels fragmentation, discontinuity, repetition and 'spiralling', denies that he is revealing the final disintegration of the Western imagination. What lies revealed, he suggests, is the disintegration of an absolute notion of Truth, and of the ability of the human intellect to discover that Truth and embody it in a work of art. Modern literature, he writes, 'denies us the comfort of finding a centre, a single meaning, a speakable truth, either in art or in the world; in its stead it gives us back a sense of the potential of each moment, each word, each gesture, each event. . .'[20] In religious education, in practice, whether inside or outside the Christian sub-culture, one depends on hints and guesses, which may be sought as fruitfully in literature as in our own private experience, or in the experience of a small group of religious thinkers who may be thought of as having tested religious concepts in their own lives at far beyond the normal level of intensity. Such hints and guesses give us some grasp on the historical depth of the religious vocabulary, and for the moment we have to be content with that. 'Like a doctor prescribing a medicine for each disease I use whatever remedy is at hand to save the world,' as Han-Shan, the T'ang poet, said.[21]

Here is an example. The French religious thinker, Simone Weil, who spent the latter part of her short life in exploring the legacy of the religious past, Classical Greek, Jewish, Christian and Buddhist, wrote in her New York Notebook: 'Leave it to God to avenge the offences we receive, offer our hatred to God: if our God is the true God the hatred in us will be burned up by contact with the Good.'[22] She meant, I suppose, that hatred, an obsession with someone else's being at all, a desire that they may be hurt, defeated, or destroyed altogether, is utterly negative as far as one's own being is concerned. If hatred succeeds in harming its object one is not thereby delivered from hatred. Nor is hatred an illness, which can be dealt with by a doctor or a psychiatrist. Most of the time it is a normal, standard human reaction to someone else's existence. Hatred obsesses, chokes, absorbs the self; from concentrated hatred only aridity develops, together with physical sensations of pain and burning, as hatred becomes a self-torment turned on the body.

Simone Weil's solution, as I interpret it, was to bring together the opposite poles of being – hatred and the true God – by whom she did not necessarily mean the Christian description of God. One should focus one's attention, hatred and all, on the centrum; not, however, as so often in the Western religious tradition, with the inner purpose of persuading God to hate as well, of manipulating his power in order to destroy what is hated, but in order to permit God to absorb the burden of one's hating, to let its negative aggression burn itself out in an opposing divine fire. One cannot resist or very much deflect one's own hatred by an act of will, but one can learn to stand aside and let the impulse flow away towards the divine.[23]

There is nothing here which can easily be taught or easily be learned, but there is a glimpse of a way of acting which might satisfy some of Wittgenstein's hesitations and make the concept of God seem less incredible. Many of today's advocates of religious education do not interest themselves in such a result, but want a method which will ensure that children internalize particular ideas of law and order; as in the 1840s religious training is seen as an answer to riot. On the other hand, any educational system which stimulates children to criticize either contemporary culture or contemporary politics runs the risk of being starved of money. Religious education ought to be part of that uncertain frontier of educational reform where reform means making sixth-form and university courses more than technological instruction with a career bias. And religious education has the disadvantage that when it rises above the familiar level of biblical technology it rapidly passes beyond the stage of life which students have reached. It is probably fortunate that religious instruction is essentially a matter for adult education.

NOTES

1. N. Smart, *Secular Education and the Logic of Religion*, Faber 1968, pp. 95–6.
2. See, for example, Jean Holm, 'The Study of Religion and RE', in *Religion*, Autumn 1980.

3. Jean Holm, art. cit., p. 212.

4. See my 'The Church and Education: an alternative view', in *Newman and Education* ed. M. Davies, Spode House 1980, p. 72.

5. H. Thielicke, *The Evangelical Faith*, ET 1977, vol 2, p. 436.

6. K. Rahner, *Hominisation*, ET 1965, from *Die Hominisation als theologische Frage*, 1958. Italics mine.

7. Rahner, op. cit., pp. 102–3.

8. It is interesting that in January 1981, for example, both the Archbishop of Canterbury (Dr Runcie) and Cardinal Hume appeared before a House of Commons Select Committee on Secondary School Curricula and Examinations, and gave evidence in favour of a spiritual ingredient in the curriculum and of some form of worship in state schools. In effect, they were pleading for the maintenance of the *status quo*.

9. L. Wittgenstein, *Culture and Value*, tr. P. Winch, Blackwell 1980, pp. 64–64e. Italics Wittgenstein's.

10. Ibid., p. 33e. Italics Wittgenstein's. This passage should be compared with the quotation from Thielicke above: the theologian (in the most traditionally Christian sense of the word) was not, of course, thinking of Wittgenstein.

11. Ibid., p. 86e.

12. See chapter 1, p. 18.

13. See chapter 8, p. 126 and chapter 2, p. 39.

14. Thomas Wright, *The Great Unwashed*, 1868, p. 92.

15. For all this, see my 'Feelings and Festivals', a study of working-class religion, in *The Victorian City* ed. H. Dyos and M. Wolff, vol 2, Routledge 1973; 'The Role of Religion in the Structure of the late Victorian City', in Trans. Royal Hist. Soc., vol 23, 1973; and chapter nine of *Holding the Fort*, Studies in Victorian Revivalism, Epworth Press 1979.

16. Wittgenstein, op. cit., p. 28e.

17. Much critical work, literary and historical, has centred on the crucial importance for modern history of the late seventeenth century. G. Josipovici, for example, in *The Lessons of Modernism*, Macmillan 1977, argued that since that time the majority of people in the West had thought of the self as a stronghold: when the self thinks, so to say, it looks inwards, shutting out external confusion. Modernism, however, has revealed that this self, which seemed so firmly rooted, was a construction, not a part of nature. And so Bunyan might be explained as part of this self-defining process, fundamental to the growth of Western individualism, which has now collapsed – it is alleged – in chaos. I suppose that in this way *Grace Abounding* becomes the religious equivalent of *Robinson Crusoe*; but the latter seems to me to be a successful attack on the kind of interventionist Puritanism in which Bunyan specialized.

18. Wittgenstein, op. cit., p. 29e. In the same passage he writes: 'Religion says: Do this – Think like that – but it cannot justify this and once it even tries to, it becomes repellent, because for every reason it offers there is a counter reason. It is more convincing to say: Think like this, however strangely it may strike you. Or, won't you do this, however repugnant you find it.'

19. F. R. Leavis, *Anna Karenina and Other Essays*, Chatto & Windus 1967, pp. 46–7. Leavis said in this essay of *Pilgrim's Progress*: 'One of the things which we learn from frequenting the great works of art is that where life is strong in any culture, the "questions" ask themselves insistently, and the "answers" change from age to age, but in some way that challenges our thought; the profound sincerity of past answers will invest them for our contemplation with a kind of persisting validity.'

20. G. Josipovici, *The Lessons of Modernism*, Macmillan 1977, p. 138.

21. From *Cold Mountain*, 100 Poems by the T'ang poet, Han-Shan, tr. Burton Watson, Jonathan Cape 1970, p. 67. A Chinese buddhist poet from perhaps the eighth or ninth centuries.

22. Simone Weil, *First and Last Notebooks*, tr. Richard Rees, OUP 1970, p. 331.

23. 'We need to be taught', Simone Weil said, 'by those who understand more and better than ourselves. For example, by Christ. . . what is it that Christ understands better than we do if not how to act: it is his judgment, his justice, which has transformed our idea of justice.'

8 Theology and Religious Studies at 16+: the Relation of School to University

John Coulson

1. Academic theology

Theology and the University emerged from a specific confessional concern with the failure of Roman Catholic theology in this country to be in any way related to the general culture, especially as that culture was formed within the universities. We felt ourselves to be outside the 'creative centre'; and in 1963 we held the sixth Downside symposium, *Theology and the University* (published in 1964) to investigate this question ecumenically. A sequel, *Theology in Modern Education*, was published in 1965. Our conclusions were not quite what we had anticipated. In those days it was still plausible to believe that we should aim at a Catholic faculty of theology running in parallel with existing faculties or departments; and no less a radical theologian than Hans Küng actually proposed this to me. What we discovered was that if theology were not to remain dead and neglected it had need of three things: 'a university setting, lay participation and the ecumenical dialogue'; and that although the teachers ought to speak out of their respective traditions, the department – its policy and its teaching – must be open.

(i) *Ecumenical dialogue.* The symposium took place in the first year of the second Vatican Council; but what was already becoming plain was the extent of the impoverishment of theology caused by Christian disunity. A better understanding of theology as an ecclesial discipline – as taking place within a community whose language it interprets – grew up alongside deeper and more eirenical conceptions of Christian membership: what was good for Catholic theology was likely to be good for Christian theology generally. The ARCIC statements have held out the promise of inter-confessional theology.

(ii) *Lay participation*. As our conceptions of Christian membership widened, so we came to see that theology, far from being confined to the clergy, positively requires to be studied and taught by laymen. To remain healthy it has to become culturally, or contextually relevant. This had led us to distinguish between the old pastoral and, therefore, systematic theology and a new kind of theology 'of the foundations' – less systematic and professionally self-enclosed. What it is called seems to depend on whether one sees it from a confessional or a secular standpoint. But what was clear is how and where to do it – in the university.

(iii) *A university setting*. Two factors determined this conclusion. The first, as expressed by Charles Davies, was that the university was the 'creative centre of our culture' and that theology must be done within that centre.[1] But why, apart from considerations of expedience, does theology belong there?

What led us to this question was the success especially of the papers and discussions on theology and literature. Here we discovered the extent to which the conceptions of theologians are effective only as they are successfully 'aimed' at experience, and that 'aiming' is a mutual, inter-disciplinary business, which theologians undertake alone at their peril.[2] But we have learned more than that. As we focus upon texts of acknowledged literary achievement which require a theological attention for their fuller critical appreciation as literature, so we see that the further question is why this should be so. What has literary achievement to do with religious insight? Does it authenticate it? It certainly takes theology back to its foundations in a common experience of the human predicament.

We have come to see that it is the questions posed from within another discipline which most fruitfully provoke theologians to develop and modify their pre-suppositions. I have cited a literary example. But even 'internal' questions of church order (the ministry, inter-communion, celibacy) are best argued out to the satisfaction of sociologists and psychiatrists, if they are to make any kind of sense – and that is what the term 'contextual relevance' was coined to express. Its use is partly justified if it makes us see that although the old conception of theology as 'queen of the sciences' is certainly wrong when interpreted in an imperial way, it still points in the right direction.

Back in the nineteenth century, F. J. A. Hort remarked that theology is peculiarly liable to corruption when it is pursued exclusively and in isolation from those disciplines which border it; and critics are rightly suspicious therefore when theologians claim that theirs is a discipline possessing the same kind of factual integrity as history, or philosophy. Such a claim would be a defensive over-reaction to the circumstances I have described, since theology cannot, of its nature, take its facts for granted as may other disciplines. Instead it can only grasp its subject matter – the Word of God as revealed – in terms of its multifarious embodiments and translations,[3] and this is why, traditionally, theology has ever been the meeting place, the unifying focus of many disciplines (exegesis, history, philosophy, law), the absence of any being destructive of the range and accuracy of the others. Disciplines have certainly claimed to be prior to others – the claim of biblical exegesis to be so, for example, has helped to divide Christendom and keeps it divided still; yet, paradoxically, the question of priority has been evaded by professional theologians, who have left it to be unconsciously determined by confessional presuppositions. The revival of interest in theological 'method' by Karl Rahner and Bernard Lonergan, for example, is a promising sign; yet even if we agree that the function of theology is the bringing of disciplines into a unifying focus, the theologian (whether he be the teacher of religion in a comprehensive school or an academic) is still open to the charge levelled at all attempts at inter-disciplinary study and teaching: that he is not a second-order discipline, but a third order one:[4] like all ideology, it does not form the judgment but selectively informs it.

The theologian usually avoids this charge – that, *qua* theologican, he will always be something of a jack-of-all-trades – by so becoming master of one that he reduces theology to philosophy, history, exegesis, or whatever second-order discipline he is qualified to profess. As I have said, this may be a form of defensiveness, since, viewed from the confessional side, the theologian still has a duty to show how the disciplines and their topics which compromise his subject matter are inter-related. Viewed from the other, the secular side, theology is part of a wider syllabus of religious studies, itself part of a comprehensive liberal education.

2. Foundations

Where there is no longer agreement on which discipline is prior to the others or on how theology may now be systematically professed, it becomes necessary to follow Karl Rahner and to go beneath theology to its foundations in experience. To do so is to encounter what Rahner terms 'the darkness of God', since our experience of life is now so fragmentary and disconnected that it is no longer able to be encapsulated in the formulations of a more self-confident age. Newman also, like

Rahner, denied that he was a 'theologian', and spoke of his books as being but propaedumata, and as offering help towards the foundations on which a fuller theology, such as may be found in the ARCIC statements, might successfully be constructed. Newman was also particularly concerned with the divorce of religion from imagination: 'It is not reason which is against us but imagination', he wrote.[5] Hence his assertion that our beliefs must first be credible to imagination before they may be convincingly professed or rationally assessed.

To set theology upon more adequate foundations is for the emphasis to be shifted from transcendence to immanence, from the deductive imposition of a tradition to its elucidation inductively. This shift may be anticipated in Newman as, in *The Idea of a University*, he moves between conceiving theology as beginning at the other end of know-ledge, as concerned not with the finite but the infinite, not with 'sensible facts' but with their Author,[6] and conceiving it as being but one element, though an essential one, of the circle of the sciences which comprise a university.[7] These aspects are not contradictory but complementary.

Such complementary emphases are also to be seen when we consider the present conduct of the purest form of deductive teaching – cate-chetics. It is defined as the systematic instruction by questioning and answer of members of a community of faith, such as is described in Acts 2.42. The faith of this family, united in prayer and worship, is expressed in doctrines which are derived from and sustain a way of life. Such theology, practised within the church, is liable to degenerate if it allows itself to become wholly internalized. Meaningful only in terms of itself, it becomes culturally irrelevant and religious teaching derived from such a self-enclosed theology cannot but be repetitive. Such a tribal or private language denies the student any prospect of enlargement through changing perspectives – hence the hostility which, in the past, catechetics aroused, especially in boarding schools, which, in addition to being schools, performed the reinforcing function of home and parish.

Such criticisms were called for in 1963. Since then, as the Theology of the Church and Sacraments syllabus testifies, for example, the form of catechesis has been modified by being opened to supplementary and examinable courses in academic theology, in which due attention is paid to adequacy of argument and, therefore, to the ability to entertain an opposite point of view at its strongest and most convincing.[8] In such schools, by regaining its regulative function, which is to bring into a unifying focus the diverse aspects of the Christian religion, theology is practised as an ecclesial discipline. This complexity arises from the fact that the central fact of Christianity is not a set of doctrines, but the incarnation. Where the philosopher seeks a divine principle, the Christian seeks a divine agent; and religion for the Christian is thus dogmatic, devotional and practical 'all at once'.[9] Such considerations apply to a greater or lesser extent to all religions, but it is especially characteristic of Christianity, whose doctrines, devotions and acts have all to be harmonized, explained and brought into equilibrium in each new generation. This, the interpretative role of theology, is essential to the well-being of the community of faith, but it degenerates if it is either obliged or permitted to become culturally self-enclosed.

The successful confessional school,[10] witnessing as it does to the fact that religion is grounded in a way of life expressive of the faith, prayer and actions of its members, assumes, therefore, a complex assent which its catechetical methods are framed to investigate. When it succeeds, it produces a sensibility in which the diverse aspects of a confessional faith are united in a healthy equilibrium. So catechized, its sixth formers should be able to navigate a middle course between simple fundamentalism and simple scepticism.

3. The secular perspective

If not before, then at 16+ catechetical theology surrenders its protected status, as its pupils re-examine the foundations of their beliefs within a new perspective. At last they meet their fellow citizens on common ground as all deepen their participation in a society which (for as long as it remains free) is and will become increasingly plural socially, politically and religiously. In the institutions which such a society maintains – whether comprehensive school or university – the self-evident truth and authority of Christianity cannot and may not be presumed. From this standpoint of a severe, secularized openness emphasis shifts from Christian theology in particular to religious studies in general.[11] It presents a change of perspective in circumstances which induce what an American theologian has called 'hermeneutical indecision'.[12] In other words we are faced with a new problem about belief – not of what to believe, but of whether we need to believe anything or to have beliefs in common. What happens, in effect, is that in the absence of an agreed metaphysic, the correction and refinement of our respective categories of interpretation become mutual; and mediating structures are created which enable this mutual correction to take place. On a small scale it is the seminar or the symposium; on a larger scale it is the comprehensive school and ultimately the university. Theology owes its seat at the table and its place in the university because of what it *has* done. It represents what has helped to form our culture historically: but also it provides a language of 'enabling', that is a language which enables us to talk about birth, puberty, marriage and death,[13] and enables symbols and festivities to continue to be realized. But theology remains in such mediating structures more on their terms than its own. It is suspect by neighbouring disciplines, such as philosophy and literary criticism, because it raises questions of truth in odd and complex ways.

Such considerations apply to a greater or lesser extent to all religions, whose complexity derives from the history and variety of activities which comprise a religion – its doctrines, its acts within history (and therefore its life as a social polity or confession), but also its scriptures, its worship and its liturgy.

Thus questions of truth in relation to a religion cannot be asked simply in terms of verifying instances; and this kind of verification (with its sceptical suspension of belief, its determination to hold nothing to be true until it is proved to be so, and its tendency to reductive explanation) must be distinguished from the mode appropriate to religion: 'Is not the proof of religion of this kind?' asks Newman in a letter: 'I liken it to the mechanism of some triumph of skill, tower or spire, geometrical staircase or vaulted roof, where Ars est celare artem; where all display of strength is carefully avoided, and the weight is ingeniously thrown in a variety of directions, upon supports which are distinct from, or independent of each other.'

I would be prepared to generalize my argument to make the following claim: the theologian's external (as distinct from internal) usefulness in a secular institution consists in his ability to deal *adequately* and in a general way with the complex phenomena of 'commitment' (or assent). It is a field he shares with philosophers and sociologists, but especially with poets and novelists; and for too long ours has been a culture which has tolerated a dangerous divorce between religion and imagination. As early as the 1840s Newman spoke of poetry as having become our mysticism,[14] and forty years later Matthew Arnold asserted that 'the strongest part of our religion today is its unconscious poetry'.[15] Conversely, a religion which ceases to be founded in imaginative assent sentences itself to death. Small wonder that it is the poets, not the preachers, who provide the children of a secular culture with its most convincing signals of transcendence.

To use imagination is to see our world differently.[16] As our standpoint or focus changes, so we gain an enlarged sense of reality. But our powers of perception are not merely enlarged. They are re-ordered. The imagination of a Shakespeare or a Dostoevsky, for example, succeeds in reconciling diversities of character and incident, and in thus bringing about 'a more than usual state of emotion with more than usual order', it gives us

> Profoundest knowledge to what point, and how,
> The mind is lord and master – outward sense
> The obedient servant of her will.

Thus to understand the function and operation of imagination in literature is to be prepared for the understanding of what is involved when the believer speaks of making a real assent to the Word of God as revealed. This is also what it is for a pupil to become 'religiate': as he sees that all forms of commitment or assent have a common factor: the extent to which they raise questions of truth within a complex structure,[17] which belongs essentially to and is inseparable from the means of its verification. Like a poem, the creed must be responded to as a whole; and a synoptic gospel can no more be reduced to a simpler form without a complete change of character than can a great tragedy.

My argument is that the theologian teaching religious studies in a comprehensive school or a university may legitimately assert that of all acts of commitment or assent, religious assent appears to be the most complex; and the pupil may be taught how to detect whether a discussion of religious assent had been sufficiently complex and had borne sufficient aspects in mind, or whether the account given was too reductive. This would, for example, characterize his approach to the accounts of religious belief given by Freud and Marx. It is like walking a tightrope and I would suggest that theologians are most in danger of falling off if they allow the impression to be formed that theological understanding can occur without some experience of commitment. Here is the danger when theology forms part of a liberal education.

By being taught 'liberally', it may end in simple scepticism, as it faces for the thousandth time the crucial question – how may I believe what I cannot satisfactorily explain or prove? This is the negative aspect; the positive is that since, as T. S. Eliot remarks, 'a higher religion is one which is much more difficult to believe',[18] we need the enemy; faith lives by dialectic; we must pass through the fiery brook or Feuerbach. The same point was made by Newman towards the end of his life when he said that 'theology makes progress by being always alive to its own fundamental uncertainties';[19] but the fact remains – a university cannot teach *for* commitment but only for its investigation. At the least it is licensed 'to inquire into'; at the most it may investigate from the side of commitment or from within an explicitly stated confessional tradition. It can do no more without compromising academic integrity. And where there is initially no commitment, or it is too feeble, the university may not provide it – and this is where collaboration with the school is of the greatest importance.

4. School and the university?

Since the aim of the confessional school is to ensure that all the aspects of a confessional faith are brought together into a healthy equilibrium, a good sixth-former should possess a religious sensibility sufficiently enriched for him to perceive the inadequacy of simple scepticism or reductive rationalism. A university department of Theology and Religious Studies will offer an alternative – either an intensification of the theological studies already begun in the sixth form, if not before, or that further widening and changing of perspectives which is effected by Religious Studies.

Such alternatives are, of course, open to all. Pupils from secular maintained schools also choose whether to develop a more systematic acquaintance with Christian theology specifically, or to continue more professionally a process, already begun, of studying religion in general or religion other than Christianity. In this latter respect some schools are ahead of some departments of theology. The contribution to religious understanding by the secular school lies in the extent to which it succeeds in becoming a living embodiment of those values which maintain a culture whose plurality is social as well as religious. As Jo Gibson has shown, it encourages the toleration of differing beliefs and of the persons professing them, by showing how beliefs inform and determine a legitimately different way of life from that which the critic takes uncritically for granted. The values thus elicited inductively by experience are neither mere opinions, nor incorrigible assertions which can never be modified, developed and adapted. A plural society and its culture are grounded in their toleration and sympathetic understanding.

5. The prospect at 16+

The prospect at 16+ is like having to chart a course between Scylla and Charybdis. I have already suggested that it may involve facing the claims of rival logics, as we are pulled one way by the deductive imposition of confessional beliefs, and another by the values which are elicited inductively by adult experience. Perhaps it is not rival logics which confront us, but rival ethics which oblige us to choose between habits of affirmation and those of sceptical suspicion. We seem to stand between two claims. For the Roman Catholic this is to be led to the issues which formed the Modernist crisis. This, in the words of von Hügel, was an extension of intensification of the perennial attempt as old as Renascence Humanism to reinterpret traditional Christian belief in the light of 'the philosophy and the scholarship and the science of the later and latest times'. One method of mental training seems at odds with the other. How do we make the transition from faith to facts; dogmas to history; and from empirical data to supernatural knowledge? Such ways of putting the dilemma led Blondel to postulate a 'two way passage between facts and faith, as it were, a going out and a coming back': 'the journey from facts to dogmas is inescapably bound up with the return journey from dogmas to facts'. Such a transition, although dialectically essential, is separable for purposes of analysis only; its elements are inseparable in the living out of our actions, which constitutes 'the practical verification of speculative truths'.[20]

Both the dilemma and the suggestions for its resolution, however, cannot be confined to Roman Catholics. Theologians from other confessions have also been faced with the problem of holding two claims in tension, which cannot be resolved into a single coherent statement. Matthew Arnold, for example, speaks of himself as living between two worlds – 'one dead, the other powerless to be born'; and of our being able to live neither without Christianity, nor with it as it is. In our own time, Dietrich Bonhoeffer has spoken of a world 'come of age', where God is not required as a working hypothesis; yet, at the same time, he opposes all efforts to reduce Christianity (in the manner of Feuerbach) to an essence: 'My view is that the full content, including the "mythological" concepts, must be kept,' he writes. The mythology is not a mere 'clothing': 'it is the thing itself'.[21] Bonhoeffer's tension between a personal 'secret discipline' and a world 'come of age' is significantly akin to that between Arnold's two worlds. Each seems to conceive the theologian's calling as, not to resolve such paradoxes, but to live through them. And perhaps this is how we should understand Kierkegaard's remark that 'the paradox is not a concession, but a category'. He adds, 'It is the duty of the human understanding to understand that there are things which it cannot understand, and what those things are.'[22] This is one side (and not the least important) of what a theologian ought to teach.

I suspect that one can detect the seeds of this paradox in Mill's juxtaposition of Bentham and Coleridge (and for teaching purposes this is where I find it most fruitful to begin). Bentham took his stand outside received opinions and institutions, Coleridge inside. For Bentham the question to ask of what we accepted was is it true, if it is true? and for Coleridge what is the truth which the continued existence of an opinion or institution implies? Our society tends to go the way of Bentham, and then to tease itself with the question: 'Can a society survive in a creatively human way without religion in any form?' As the quality of life appears to go down, so the question tends to take a sharper form: If you deny, abolish, or ignore religious belief, what takes its place? Something better? – because less complex and demanding? Something natural? – how mild a virus is 'hermeneutical indecision'? Or something toxic? – does another discipline (like literature or philosophy) suffer, if it finds itself in the place left vacant by theology?

I should hope that a theologian would intervene to say that he had been taught both to recognize that complex act of inference and assent on which his discipline depends, and to keep such questions open, by living with their uncertainties and paradoxes. He might even go so far as to claim that in thus dispelling the imperial pretensions of theology, he was revealing the catalytic function of religion. If it is to possess a sufficient stability, a plural society positively requires citizens who have been taught to conduct investigations under the control of and for the sake of their beliefs. What a university theology teaches is a *method* by which the two diverse claims and their separate cultures – the deductive imposition, by catechesis, of a confessional faith, and the inductive experience of the values which maintain a plural society – can at least be brought to bear upon each other, and even occasionally reconciled. This theology is liberal in that its method requires that both its neighbouring disciplines and those of which it is composed are harmonized without their integrity as disciplines being compromised.[23] Such a theology, hermeneutically 'decisive', yet always open to further questions, also provides the believer with the means by which his faith may survive in a society which still respects and tolerates what it no longer explicitly professes.

NOTES

1. Charles Davies, 'Theology and its present task', *Theology and the University*, DLT 1964, pp. 108–9. This conception of the university is compatible with, if not derived from, that which is so much insisted upon by F. R. Leavis.

2. David Jenkins, in *Theology and the University*, p. 219: 'For example, the theologian (simply as a man) may be struck by a note of despair and monotony deeply felt and deeply moving in the work of Samuel Becket. He must *not* cut that despair and monotony 'down to size' by a facile application of categories from his customary talk about sin, redemption and forgiveness. Rather he must face up, as a man who is one with those for whom Becket speaks, in the human situation, to the reality and authenticity, to the dimension, of this despair. And *then* he must seek to shape his understanding and systematization of, say, the Doctrine of Redemption and of the new life in Christ in such a way as to speak relevantly to, and take undiminished account of, the reality and validity of the despair experienced and

expressed. Only thus will he be at all true to the theological insight that in Christ there is a new creation (2 Cor. 5).'

3. See chapter 4, p. 72 (Jamison).

4. Cf. John Macquarrie in chapter 11. Despite the differences in their use of these categories, both papers are concerned with the way in which theology may explain and order the experience on which it is based: and John Coulson is concerned with the extent to which theology is an inter-disciplinary study (Ed.).

5. Newman's *Letters and Diaries* XXIX, Clarendon Press.

6. Image ed. 395; 0.350, Doubleday, NY.

7. It is interesting that Newman took this view in one of the *Lectures on the Scope and Nature of University Education*, which he delivered in Dublin in 1852 – a passage which he did not feel able to republish! 'The assemblage of sciences . . . may be said to be *in equilibrio* as long as all its portions are secured to it. Take away one of them, and that one is important in the catalogue as Theology, and disorder and ruin at once ensue. There is no middle state between *equilibrium* and chaotic confusion; one science is ever pressing upon another, unless kept in check; and the only guarantee of truth is the cultivation of them all. And such is the office of the University.'

8. See chapter 6, p. 97.

9. *Oxford University Sermons* 28–9. *Essay on Development*, I.1.3.

10. This is written from a background of long existence of the school and community at Downside. See also chapter 3, p. 50 (Ed.).

11. See chapter 2, p. 37.

12. A. McGill, 'The Ambiguous position of Christian Theology', in *The Study of Religion in Colleges and Universities* ed. Paul Ramsey and John F. Wilson, Princeton University Press 1970.

13. See chapter 2, p. 39.

14. *Essays Critical and Historical*, i 291.

15. In *Essays in Criticism*, 1865.

16. Cf. Bernard Lonergan's description of the effect of the fifth functional speciality, conversion, which is 'as if one's eyes were opened and one's former world faded and fell away' (*Method in Theology*, DLT 1972, p. 103).

17. See chapter 4, p. 71.

18. T. S. Eliot, *Notes Towards the Definition of Culture*, Faber 1948, p. 67.

19. Newman's *Letters and Diaries* XXXIX, Clarendon Press, p. 118.

20. Maurice Blondel, *History and Dogma*, Harvill Press 1964, p. 274.

21. Dietrich Bonhoeffer, *Letters and Papers from Prison*, The Enlarged Edition, SCM Press 1971, pp. 326, 329.

22. Kierkegaard, *Journals*, 1847, Alexander Dru, Herperford Books, NY 1959, pp. 117–18.

23. Cf. chapter 9, p. 159.

9 The Study of Theology in University and School

Stephen Sykes

I

The starting point for this paper must clearly be the contributions to the 1964 Downside Symposium, *Theology and the University*, edited by John Coulson. In this volume, Christopher Butler, writing before the end of the second session of the Second Vatican Council, set the tone by arguing for the desirability of an authentically Roman Catholic contribution to the normal theological study of English universities. The ecumenical intention of this argument was undergirded by six contributions, which confirmed John Coulson's remark that 'the English opportunity for Catholics and non-Catholics to collaborate within an open department of theology has no parallel elsewhere and is therefore uniquely ecumenical' (pp. 3–4). The ecumenical contribution is specifically found in the analyses of existing practice in British Universities from Professor Reid, of Aberdeen, David Jenkins, of Oxford, and Professor Richardson, of Nottingham.

The necessity of three contributions is notable, reflecting the differences between locally negotiated traditions. Thus the practice of theology in Scotland is dominated by the establishment of the Church of Scotland, and the presence on academic appointing committees of a proportion of Church of Scotland representatives. (This historic fact, which, indeed, Professor Reid neither mentions nor seeks to justify, did not prevent the University of Edinburgh from recently appointing in Professor J. R. Mackey, a married Roman Catholic priest, to the Chair of Divinity; nor did the apparent ecumenism, or at least openness, of this appointment prevent a number of Church of Scotland dignitaries from expressing scandal and dismay.) Professor Reid's contribution is, in effect, an uncompromising statement of the Protestant biblical tradition. It offers no vision of an ecumenical strengthening of that tradition, and regrets only the isolation of theology from the social sciences (in effect, the isolation of the social sciences from theology).

David Jenkins describes the founding and development of the Oxford Honour School of Theology, from 1868 onwards. He describes the painful process of de-confessionalization, whereby Anglican interests, presuppositions and doctrinal norms ceased to dominate the examination and (in due course) the structure and content of the syllabus. This is a process to which I attach the greatest importance, and therefore is one of which I shall want to speak later. Jenkins' criticism of contemporary theology at Oxford is, however, significant. It is not, he says 'constructive enough for believers and not open and relevant enough for unbelievers' (p. 159). Theological study ought, he argues, to go beyond history and philosophical analysis into systematics; not the systematics of the 'master-theologian', but of an explorer and a servant. 'A liberated and open theology free from the sheltered indoctrination of the seminary is necessary for the layman and necessary for the communication of the Church with the world; and, if this is so, it is a necessity also for the priest. And it may well be that it is in the severe openness of a secular university that this sort of theology can be alone worked out' (p. 162). John Coulson points out the paradoxical consequence that precisely in the context of such theological openness, 'it is not only permissible but necessary that its teachers should make their denominational position as clear as possible' (p. 4).

Professor Richardson, speaking from the context of a university without a denominational past, shows how the admissability of a department of theology in a university depended upon the theologian's acceptance of the practice of the historical method. Precisely this feature made it suspect to Tractarian Anglicans of Pusey's type, to conservative evangelicals, and (until comparatively recently) to Roman Catholics. But with the waning of the dominance of a false ideal of 'scientific history', interpretative construction of the history of theology became more respectable. The controversial subjects of dogmatics, apologetics, liturgiology and ethics become teachable where an effort is made to see them from a variety of points of view. Appointments to the staff of an open university must, however, not be denominationally controlled.

In this connection Richardson observes that 'the situation in the universities is not basically different from that in the state-supported schools' (p. 170). Indeed the 1944 Act has created, he notes, a demand for lay teachers of religious knowledge met largely by the theology departments of the modern universities. Richardson, like Jenkins, is partly critical of the present situation, and is acquainted with (but disapproves of) proposals to substitute departments of religion for departments of theology. He calls for a stronger development of theological options in general degrees, and for departments of the History of Ideas in modern universities shy of introducing a full-blooded honours theology course.

Richardson's appraisal of the situation in 1963 seems to be both perceptive and prophetic. John Coulson rightly remarks that since the universities for which Richardson speaks were neutral in matters of religion, 'Catholics can be accepted on equal terms with other denominations' (p. 5). However, in one respect the article (indeed the whole book) is deficient; that is, in relation to the astonishing development of 'religious studies', pioneered largely by Professor Ninian Smart at Lancaster. For the briefest reference to this, we must turn to a caveat in the form of a note by Professor Hilary Armstrong of the University of Liverpool, a Roman Catholic layperson and Professor of Greek. Christians who seek for a new department of theology in a university must, he says, ask themselves in what respect such a depart-ment is, or is not, conceived of as a 'centre of Christian propaganda rather than of properly academic teaching and research' (p. 189). To define theology in the latter sense may involve studying in an objective and scholarly manner the complete range of Christian beliefs and practices with a view not to 'teaching doctrine', but 'showing what doctrine is'. And with a reference to Ninian Smart, Armstrong asks whether, in this context, serious consideration ought not to be given to expansion of the curriculum to include the study of other religions. Smart is quoted to the effect that 'it is precisely when, in a Department of Religion, theology is liable to be subjected to the need to respond to the challenges of humanism, Marxism, and the like, that serious theology gets done.'[1]

One is bound to remark that this brief comment strikes a powerful note of realism in the somewhat cosy discussion of courses of study in the well-established departments of theology. In view of the terms of reference of the symposium it could hardly have been otherwise. As far as the participation of Roman Catholics in university departments of theology is concerned we are, in 1963, in very early days; and there are signs of a certain protectiveness. Butler seems to think that there is some practical way of ensuring the presence of what he calls 'genuinely Catholic theology' without raising the awkward principle of the external control of appointments (p. 20). Francis Davis writes of the dangers to young Catholic students in a department entirely composed of 'liberal' theologians, and adds with some satisfaction that 'the majority of lecturers in a university theology department are orthodox Christians' (p. 180). In Lawrence Bright's mostly admirable proposals for teaching theology in an English University, the suggestion is made that it would be a reasonable safeguard in an ecumenical department of theology for each student to have a tutor of his or her own denomination (p. 279). Not only have none of these safeguards actually transpired in even the well-established departments of theology, the actual terms of future discussion were more accurately foreseen by Armstrong. In one striking case, namely Cambridge, the department has entirely thrown off all Anglican denominational control of appointments, incorporated the study of religion in its terms of reference, and appointed to a chair of philosophy of religion a married Roman Catholic priest who is a powerful opponent of recent disciplinary measures against nonconforming Roman Catholic theologians.

The key to this situation is the impossibility of imagining any acceptable form of the denominational control of appointments. Since the universities are funded by public money, as Richardson put it, 'it is unthinkable that credal tests of any kind should ever again be imposed as a qualification for university entrance' (p. 169). And what applies to university entrance applies, *a fortiori*, to university appointments. There is, in fact, no way of ensuring a good ecumenical mix, and no way of removing a university teacher who changes his or her denomination, or who lapses from Christian profession altogether. Rightly, appointments are not controlled by the existing members of a department, so that the quality of a candidate for a given post may prevail over all other considerations. Departmental traditions are fragile, and with staff turnover, syllabuses themselves may change. A 1980 Cambridge degree in Theology and Religious Studies may bear no relation whatever to a theology degree taken fifteen years earlier. This is the reality of the new environment which any modern comment on existing practice must recognize.

In emphasizing the changes one must recognize, likewise, both the charity and the integrity of the 1963 symposiasts. In his introduction, John Coulson employs a phrase which he takes to encapsulate the ideal department of theology, expressed by Jenkins, Richardson, Francis Davis, and Bright; 'an open department but committed men' (p. 5). With the qualification noted above about the impossibility of ensuring particular commitments, this phrase nonetheless has an entirely modern ring about it. Edward Hulmes, in his recent argument for regarding personal commitment as a primary resource in religious education, nonetheless insists that Christian teachers be self-aware and self-critical.[2] 'Openness' in this context means the establishment of an internal and external dialectic between contrary views. Nothing in Hulmes' admirable prescriptions for the conduct of religious education is inapplicable to a theology department fashioned on the 1963 symposiasts' principles. As Jenkins put it, in reaction to the false triumphalism or opportunism of the past, 'we have somewhat lost our grasp upon the fact that we have a special position not of privilege but of responsibility' (p. 160).

It is, moreover, not merely in respect of the *theory* of theological education that *Theology and the University* has made an impressive contribution. It is apparent to any observer of British universities that the Roman Catholic contribution has grown in self-confidence, and that, in particular, in many departments of theology there is an obvious presence of Roman Catholic students. In Durham, for example, where we have the advantage of the physical presence of the largest Roman Catholic seminary in the country, seminarians combine with Roman Catholic students, both male and female, to create a natural dialectic with the assumptions and methods of either Anglican or German Protestant critical orthodoxy. It is in the last two decades, also, that certain major Roman Catholic systematicians, such as Rahner, Küng, Schillebeeckx, and Lonergan have made outstanding contributions to the ecumenical character of theology by their readiness to hold dialogue with Protestant, or at least non-Roman Catholic, biblical scholarship, systematics and philosophy. This same development has, if I am not mistaken, isolated a certain strand of Anglicanism which, for all its virtues of independent-mindedness, has, as I shall hope to illustrate, fallen prey to the startling inadequacies of English theological education.

II

My next task is, accordingly, to attempt a new, or at least revised picture of developments in English theological education. Previous accounts have perhaps suffered from a certain native parochialism. It would, of course, be grossly unfair to charge David Jenkins with such a restricted outlook, since he quite explicitly intended to restrict himself to speaking about the Oxford Theology School. However, even Oxford exists in a wider context, and in order adequately to understand Oxford one must, I believe, set theological education in a Western European environment.

From such a perspective, two important, but neglected points become obvious. The first is that the dominant tradition to which Western Christendom is heir is that the study of theology is an ecclesial discipline. It is important to remind the modern English academic that some of the finest examples of theological writing exist in the form of sermons or of prayers. Moreover, virtually all the major contributions, to the contemporary theological environment have been made by those writing in the context of confessionally committed institutions of higher education, whether universities, institutes, academies or seminaries. In particular in the West, we are heirs to a highly developed tradition of confessional apologetics, the inheritance of the Reformation. Because the division between Protestant and Roman Catholic is represented as existing at epistemological level or at the level of fundamental theology, there is scarcely any theological topic which does not exhibit in one way or another the result of basic confessional options.

The second, similarly neglected point emerges as a qualification of the first. European theological scholarship, in origin confessional and frequently apologetic, has been experiencing in the last one hundred years a process of de-confessionalization. This process is regionally variable, depending on the extent to which the substance of a particular confession has penetrated a given culture. The sociological interpretation of this process is complex, but the contribution of theological scholarship to it is plain enough. It is rooted, as Professor Richardson observed, in the European historical movement, and it has permeated the primary sub-disciplines of theological scholarship, namely, research, interpretation and history. In this way it has considerably undermined the inferior, apologetically-oriented histories of the biblical period and of the church, and created a partly deconfessionalized European community of theological scholars.

The character of this Western theological common market can be further clarified by reference to Lonergan's outline of the theological disciplines. These constitute a 'set of related and recurrent operations cumulatively advancing towards an ideal goal'. There are two phases; the first tells you what theologians of the past have said, while the second confronts the questions of today. In the first phase, the discipline of research strives to apprehend the data, the discipline of interpretation seeks insight into the data, and the discipline of history judges and discriminates between the various theories put forward to account for the data. These three disciplines culminate in a bridge discipline, which Lonergan terms dialectic, which deals with the conflicts occurring within Christian movements, comparing and criticizing their outcomes and acknowledging the force of any vital decisions which must be made. In Lonergan's scheme the four disciplines of the first phase lead to four disciplines in the second, constructive phase, which he terms foundations, doctrines, systematics and communications. The total eightfold division, it should be remembered, is a pattern of *related* and *recurring* operations. Decisions taken in the context of dialectics and foundations, do, therefore, tend to permeate the whole. Despite the ecumenical potential in the disciplines of the first phase, de-confessionalization of theological scholarship even at these levels is not fully realizable.

This description of the kinds of specialization which exist within theology, a description itself sensitive to the change from a classicist to an empirical notion of culture, helps greatly to place modern developments in context. What, in effect, has occurred in English departments of theology is that the second phase disciplines have been abandoned, and theological study has come to be identified with the four disciplines in the first phase, namely, research, interpretation, history and dialectic. Organizationally, the second phase has been assigned to the separate theological colleges of the different denominations. Here the aim is explicitly to produce those who communicate, in word or symbolic deed, the substance of the Christian gospel. The disciplines of doctrine and systematics, which manifestly belong to the life and mission of the Christian church have languished uneasily, half-claimed by university practitioners of the history of doctrine, and often inadequately taught in theological colleges. The serious problem of the interconnection of both phases has left a legacy of uncertainty as to whether or not theology is an appropriate discipline in a secular university setting.

The precise stages and consequences of deconfessionalization can, however, be studied in somewhat closer detail. In England (I am not able to do justice to Scotland at this point), the first university to pioneer a theological degree course was the University of Durham, from its origins in 1832. Here, as subsequently in both Oxford and Cambridge, theological study *meant* Anglican theology, with strong emphasis on the Bible (because of Article VI), on the fathers of the undivided church, on the study of the Thirty-Nine Articles and on the liturgy of the Book of Common Prayer. This course of study was not conceived narrowly. The liturgy lectures of Durham's first Professor of Divinity, Henry Jenkyns, for example, were notable for their breadth of view and of scholarship, the lectures being based on the researches of the seventeenth century Italian liturgiologist, Cardinal Bona.

It was the very breadth and reasonableness of this vision which enabled English universities formally to dismantle the Anglican confessional basis of the curriculum without the apparent need to start again from scratch. No justification is apparently needed for studying the scriptures (if not the Apocrypha); Dogmatic Theology to AD 451 can become, by the merest stroke of the pen, Patristics or Early Church

Doctrine; the reformation can be assimilated to the study of general church history, and the prayer book to general liturgiology. Only the Thirty-Nine Articles had to be dropped entirely, and not a few Anglicans were willing to see this apparently inferior product of the half-forgotten Anabaptist and Roman controversies of the sixteenth century relegated to the Anglican colleges.

The result: a theological syllabus, covertly but not blatantly Anglican in character capable of being taught by a body of lecturers largely consisting of Anglicans in tied chairs, tied college deaneries and chaplaincies, to generations of undergraduates, including a decent number of broadminded non-Anglicans. This was the syllabus I was taught in the late 1950s in Cambridge. It included Hebrew and Greek, Biblical Studies of Old and New Testament, Patristics, and optional Reformation Studies and Philosophy of Religion. It would be tempting, but uninstructive to deride the insufficiency of such a syllabus as a theological education; it is not even relevant to note that I was taught to despise both Barth and Bultmann, and to venerate Streeter and Kelly; it perhaps does not even matter much that I read not a word of Tillich, of Brunner, of Temple, of Maurice, of Newman or of Schleiermacher; nor would I have known to what the word hermeneutics referred. Much more serious was the fact that my theological environment had been organized for me by a locally negotiated compromise of the nature of which I was unaware. Uncovering the hidden confessional assumptions of the syllabus was, in due course, a revelation. What I subsequently discovered was that in effect I was learning, or being taught, on two quite different levels. On the surface I was assimilating data and interpretative techniques enabling me to write historical essays on widely divergent moments in the history of Israel and of the Christian church. Underneath I was somewhat desperately trying to piece together some coherent views about sin and Christ and the sacraments, from the almost random chunks of special knowledge I had about Paul, or Augustine, or Calvin, or Kant. And, moreover, I knew that my teachers had more or less coherent views on those central doctrinal questions, and were prepared to communicate them in coded messages dealing with Paul, or Augustine, or Calvin, or Kant, if only I could grasp the key.

By deconfessionalizing the theological curriculum, an unnatural theological vacuum was created. Because neither doctrine nor systematics could be taught in the direct confessional idiom of the whole of Christian history, various substitutes had to be invented by means of which the natural hunger of the theological appetite could be appeased. These substitutes have had tremendous currency in English theological circles, and deserve to be identified and unmasked. I name them, therefore, as 'biblical theology', 'dogmatic theology', 'modern theology', and 'philosophical theology'. A word must be said about each.

'Biblical theology' emerged in England as the English version of the anti-liberal movement in continental Protestantism associated with the names of Barth and Brunner. It was powerfully promoted from platforms in the English universities both by biblical scholars such as Professor C. F. D. Moule, and by theologians such as Professor Alan Richardson. Under the chairmanship of Archbishop Michael Ramsey, it was celebrated in a 1958 Lambeth Conference Report as providing God's answer to contemporary distress.

Even at the time the programme of 'biblical theology' had its critics. Under the guidance of the colourful personality of J. S. Bezzant I was brought up to believe that the genuine fundamentalist had a much clearer perception of the real situation, once the doctrine of verbal inspiration had been successfully challenged, than had the so-called 'biblical theologians'. The latter, Bezzant argued, often subconsciously assumed something like biblical fundamentalism, so fearful were they that liberalism had eviscerated the Gospel; and he criticized the 'extensive and sometimes strained selectiveness' with which they put forward what they asserted to be 'the biblical view' of the world and man.[3] 'Biblical theology' continues, however, to fill the vacuum created by the absence of the study of doctrinal theology. The continued polemics devoted to the subject of crypto-fundamentalism, and the rather tiresome invocation of the name of Ernst Troeltsch, is evidence, if of nothing else, of the continuing importance of distinguishing between biblical study and the constructive tasks of doctrinal theology. The peril of modernizing Jesus, to which H. J. Cadbury referred, consists not in the theological insistence that Jesus is risen and present with the community, but in the unconscious pressure, exerted on New Testament scholars by a church bereft of systematic theologians, to give them a portrait of Jesus who answers, implicitly or explicitly, all the questions of belief and practice which have arisen from modern man. But these are subjects for a developed doctrinal theology and theological ethics, not merely for a historian of Christian origins. Inescapably 'biblical theology' is inadequate as a substitute for doctrinal theology; though here I would like to indicate my equal conviction both that doctrinal theologians have to take sides on matters raised by biblical study, and that there is every reason why biblical scholars should insist that their work be taken with the highest seriousness by those who make doctrine their business.

The second substitute, 'dogmatic theology', I have already identified as arising out of the Anglican acceptance of the authority of the undivided church. A study of examination questions set in Oxford in the Dogmatic Theology paper shows, towards the end of the nineteenth century, the impact of the increasingly objective study of the patristic period and the end of the era when patristics were used, selectively, as ammunition in doctrinal, especially ecclesiological, argument. In 1905 the paper was retitled 'The history of Christian doctrine to AD 451'. As a result hundreds of theological students complete their studies under the impression that with the Council of Chalcedon, disagreement in christology came to an end. Some explanation is needed, I believe, for the opinion repeatedly advanced in *The Myth of God Incarnate*[4] that incarnational theology exists in one, standard form, capable of summary in a dozen words and dismissal in scarcely more.

Despite the patristic learning of the past 'Dogmatic theology' is not, and has not been for many years, a popular substitute for genuine systematics. The radical 1970 reforms of the Cambridge Tripos swept patristics away as a compulsory paper, and generations of theologians can now plunder Forsyth, Rahner and Pannenberg for christological opinions, unencumbered by any instruction in Athanasius, Nestorius or Cyril. This new form of innocence replaces the perhaps more dangerous delusion that no justification needed to be offered for considering certain councils more authoritative than others. It is as if Newman had never lived. It does not require special gifts of insight to observe in the theological formation of the older generation of theologians the remains of the long Anglican tradition of deference to the fathers, and toleration of ignorance of the scholastics. An instinctively patristic concept of the 'natural standard of orthodoxy' continues to inform even the theological radicalism of contemporary England, to the amazement of continental and North American Protestants.

The status of 'modern theology', a subject which has appeared in various guises in recent curriculum reforms, is a little more ambiguous. Sometimes the historical character of the study is emphasized by the inclusion of dates; sometimes the more systematic intention of the course is brought out by the reference made to a number of major modern theologians whose works are commended for special study; sometimes the aim of the course is clarified (some might say confused) by a reference to 'religious life and thought'. It is evident that a number of different kinds of study are being recommended under one guise. In the first place there is the history of religious thought, which is conducted chiefly by reference to major thinkers acknowledged by the contemporary world as important. Thus Kierkegaard would be included in a review of the nineteenth century, despite the fact that his work was hardly known outside Denmark until the twentieth century. Secondly, there is the history of religious life, that is, of the social phenomena of religion in the life of a society, which (we ought to have learnt from Troeltsch) cannot be separated from the study of history of thought, and which should not be detached from the study of history itself. In both those cases the impulse for study, and the methods employed derive from historiography, in the first case from the history of ideas and in the second from history itself. In neither case is it satisfactory that 'religion' be isolated from its context, and the highly demanding requirements of both the relevant general historical disciplines should not be shirked in favour of some domesticated theological version of them. It is only when they are studied in their integrity as historical subjects that their significance for doctrinal theology becomes plain; just as it is only when Christian origins are studied in close association with this history of first century religion that their significance emerges for doctrine. It is precisely the instinct to substitute what ought to be conceived as historical study to fill the vacuum created by the absence of doctrinal theology which robs these subjects of their true impact.

In the case of 'modern theology' however, there is a good reason for this substitution. For it is the careful study of the modern period which provides the student with one of the best opportunities for reflecting on the consequences for theological study of the massive intellectual changes which have overtaken traditional ways of carrying out the task of 'doctrinal theology'. One cannot, for example, conceive how the close study of Tillich or of Barth could be carried out without close attention to the crisis of theological methods which they attempted to resolve in different ways, a crisis which has its roots alike in the intellectual world of post-Kantian Germany and of the toils of a modern industrial democracy. To sever the study of these major theologians from this context is to emasculate them; and it is because of this danger that the study of 'modern theology' must be preserved from being turned into a substitute for doctrinal theology. But again it must be made clear that the doctrinal theologian needs the work of the student of the history of modern theology, and must face its challenges. Otherwise he will remain innocent of any profounder understanding of the situation which he himself is addressing. It is, of course, no accident that all the major figures (especially Tillich and Barth) whose works are considered worthy of careful study were themselves able students of history of recent theology. Nor is it surprising if their constructive work can be successfully accused of failing to meet the challenges to a contemporary theology, that this weakness is abundantly evident in their accounts of recent theological history.

The final inadequate substitute for doctrinal theology to which I have referred is 'philosophical theology'. By 'philosophical theology' I am referring to that philosophical cultivation of the themes of Christian theology at one remove from their context in Christian doctrine. For illustration one has only to consider the literature on those subjects, which, since the eighteenth century, have been widely regarded as belonging to the very essence of religion, namely, God, immortality and human freedom. That God could be discussed apart from the context of the Christian doctrine of the revelation in Christ, immortality apart from the Christian doctrine of the *Visio Dei*, and the religious significance of human freedom apart from grace and the sacraments, was considered axiomatic. It still comes as a surprise to some philosophers when Christian theologians challenge this assumption, and insist that philosophical account be taken of these ideas in the context in which they actually occur in Christian theology as a whole.

But for many who studied theology at universities the work done under the various courses investigating the relations of philosophy and religion (and by 'religion', it was not infrequently assumed, with typically Western myopia, that the Christian religion must be intended) was their only approach to the problems of Christian theology in a genuinely modern and critical frame of reference. The trouble was that the actual centre of theology was missing. Students found themselves helplessly trying to fill in the gap between their knowledge of Deutero-Isaiah and Paul on the one hand and their exposure to Hume or Kant on the other; or between Augustine and Calvin, and Wittgenstein and Ryle. They found themselves wrestling with problems of prayer, providence, miracle, life after death and so on without any sophisticated awareness of how these themes were handled in the context of an articulate and consistent expression of the Christian doctrines of creation, of election, of the last things, or even of christology, soteriology and the doctrine of the church. On these subjects their knowledge was likely to be confined to what they had picked up in the course of their historical studies; and, unless these had been turned into substitutes for their lack of knowledge of doctrinal theology, they were more likely to have been perceived as a very partial and broken series of glimpses into certain historical periods, not in any way necessarily reflecting the peculiar problems of the modern theologian.

We may summarize our findings hitherto as follows: theology as studied in English departments of theology is frequently composed of the basic disciplines (research, interpretation and history) of a partly de-confessionalized curriculum, in which the confessional vacuum is filled by a number of inadequate substitutes. The departments naturally vary in the selection of snippets from the Christian tradition which they offer to students, but deprived of the possibility of offering the traditional justification for theology study, namely the fulfilment of the Christian mission, they naturally fall back on locally acceptable justifications. Biblical study requiring ancient languages is a discipline like the study of the classics. Church history is like a specialized branch of history. The history of doctrine is like intellectual history. The analytic study of theological doctrine is like philosophy. Inevitably, when the justification for the discipline derives from the practice outside a theological environment, the coherence of the theological education suffers. The study of theology becomes a kind of general degree, in which the student acquires some, but not much, competence in languages, history, the history of ideas and philosophy.

The criticism of this state of affairs must be severe, and we have reason to be anything but complacent. Although in theory it ought to have worked to theology's advantage that the methods of study were derived from non-theological disciplines,[5] we know it to be otherwise. Biblical studies, church history, the history of doctrine and philosophy of religion have each developed their internal, cosy traditions and have been exceptionally slow to respond to outside developments. But the most severe failing, I think, is the spiritual impoverishment to which the syllabuses have condemned generations of students. Because their framers could see no way in which to combine the non-confessional stance of the public universities with the vibrantly confessional character of most centuries of Christian profession, academic respectability was formally purchased at the cost of what came, ambiguously, to be called 'relevance'. 'Relevance' sometimes meant the provision of high-class rationalization of religious prejudices. But more often, I think, it referred to desire for greater profundity in the exploration of the spiritual malaise of Western society, the themes of tragedy, forgiveness and the nature and limits of personal responsibility, all of which are central to the Christian doctrine of the *deus crucifixus*.

What is missing is patently the study of the central substance of the Christian faith, that which makes it all intellectually, morally and religiously appealing to living persons in the contemporary world.[6] But here the English department of theology meets an impasse. It is precluded from assuming the role of a denominational institution and teaching a confessional theology; ecumenical theology is an abstraction, and one open to the identical objections of propagandist partiality. Has it, then, to avoid the difficulty altogether, and advise suitably motivated candidates to satisfy their hunger privately, or at the hands of denominational chaplains or colleges?

My answer to this question is to refer once again to Lonergan's pattern of theological disciplines, and to the fourth of the first phrase of theological specialisms, namely dialectic. Lonergan's explanation of what is involved is typically dense, but includes a helpful clarification of the relationship of dialectic to the earlier disciplines of research, interpretation and history. These, he says,

> approach but do not achieve an encounter with the past. They make the data available, they clarify what was meant, they narrate what occurred. Encounter is more. It is meeting persons, appreciating the values they represent, criticizing their defects, and allowing one's living to be challenged at its very roots by their words and by their deeds. Moreover such an encounter is not just an optional addition to interpretation and history. Interpretation depends on one's self-understanding; the history one writes depends on one's horizon; and encounter is the one way in which self-understanding and horizon can be put to the test.[7]

Dialectic has to do with the conflicts that occur in Christian history in their challenges to the self-understanding, indeed the very personhood of the investigator. There is, in Lonergan's description of the task, a moral and spiritual dimension to it. 'It will provide the open-minded, the serious, the sincere with the occasion to ask themselves some basic questions, first, about others but eventually, even about themselves.'[8] By continuously facing the student with those who have differed from each other, and by critical examination of the validity of the differences, a self-scrutiny is promoted 'that can lead to a new understanding of oneself and one's destiny'.

'*Can* lead'. Nothing in dialectic, so conceived, imposes the authority of an ecclesiastical dogma or body. Although much in the secondary studies of the basic data of theology is redolent of the Christian convictions of the writers, the student's sensitivity is increasingly alerted to the nature of such commitments precisely by dialectic. This perhaps explains Lonergan's conviction that dialectic is not an optional extra in the first phase of theological disciplines. Yet, if my study of the situation in English departments of theology has any cogency, it is dialectic which is so frequently missing, to the moral and spiritual impoverishment of the student. Dimly aware of unmet needs, but lacking any coherent model or plan in which to locate the missing element, the departments have allowed the various substitutes to do inadequate duty. A less parochial analysis of the modern history of theological education, combined with the broader perspective provided by Lonergan's description of method in theology, points the way to a fruitful advance.

III

The interpretation of the recent history of religious education in schools is likewise illuminated by the foregoing analysis. The whole Western tradition of Christian theology invites Christians to conceive of the religious education of the young in terms of catechesis, that is, the instruction of the religiously immature, young or old, in the essentials of the Christian mission as conceived by a particular church at a particular time.

Two parallel influences served to emancipate schools from this tradition in England, the forces of de-confessionalization and of the independent, phenomenological study of religion. The 1944 Act is largely the product of de-confessionalization. It focusses on those aspects of Christian theological study which can apparently be pursued without denominational bias. I say 'apparently' because there were always those who argued that fundamental decision of a denominational kind had an influence upon even the first phase of the theological disciplines; Lonergan's pattern of *recurring* operations explains why this is, in fact, the case. The development of 'religious studies' is a direct result of the 'history of religions' school of thought, combined with the philosophical school of phenomenology. Its claim is that one can and should, study religions sympathetically, allowing the observation of what actually happens to prevail over the participant's prescription of what ought to be happening. It is the product of Western 'historical-mindedness', and has itself contributed largely to the forces of de-confessionalization by creating a less controversial and partisan back-cloth for the interpretation of inter-Christian religious differences.

In the secularized context of modern Britain, the theory of the study of religion, as formulated in the modern departments of religion and their earlier counterparts in Holland and elsewhere (it is a parochial mistake to attribute its foundation to Lancaster) appealed to the dominant Libertarian-pluralist ideology of popular culture. Christianity, in this scheme of thought, constitutes a minority religion in a culture which as a whole encourages a wide variety of religious and ethical life-styles. Religious education is tolerable, on these assumptions, only if it exhibits the options from which children can choose.

The current situation in religious education thus demonstrates a spectrum of view and practices, ranging from overt catechetics in church schools, the partly deconfessionalized practice of the 1944 Act, to the whole-hearted adoption of a new theoretical justification for the study of religion, and all stations in between.

The distinction which manifestly exists between schools and universities in relation to the content of syllabuses needs further explanation. Schools have moved further from the structure and content of the more conservative theological departments' syllabuses for two basic reasons. First, the schools have to provide their RE curriculum for the religious education of virtually an entire population. University departments of theology, on the other hand, have found it possible to keep going on a sufficient intake of volunteers, who study the subject with, for the most part, conspicuous diligence. Secondly, there is the not inconsiderable difference of age and maturity. The startling evidence produced by Dr Francis[9] of deteriorating attitudes towards religion from the age of eleven onwards may be quite closely connected with the conspicuous Christian absence from a largely autonomous youth culture. The monuments of Christian tradition have, for the most part, to do with persons, events and circumstances apparently at a considerable remove from the themes of modern Western youth culture. RE in school is virtually forced to have dealings with this culture; the churches, with local exceptions, think they can afford to stay aloof. An explanation of this kind is, I regret to say, no more than a guess; and the evidence to support it is, at this stage, hardly more than anecdotal. There ought, however, to be research done into the attitudes of students reading theology at university; my impression is that they are a psychologically distinguished group, at once serious-minded and emotionally immature.

What, then, are the results of this investigation? First, that a university theological course unable or unwilling to offer a discipline corresponding to what Lonergan termed 'dialectic' is a deeply impoverished one. Moreover, we have to recognize that large numbers of persons who studied theology in earlier times have suffered from such an inadequate formation, including the baleful effects of various substitutes which have been peddled.

Secondly, there is every reason to be confident that theological study, in its first phase (as defined by Lonergan), can be properly pursued in state-supported institutions of education, primary or secondary or tertiary, in such a way as not to constitute Christian propaganda conducted at public expense. At the same time, at an appropriate point, the study of dialectic must exhibit the conflicts which occur within Christianity, and which have affected even the research, interpretation and writing of history in varying degrees.

Thirdly, teachers of theology in universities ought to be alert to the opportunities of providing support and encouragement to teachers of religious studies in schools; especially in respect of that kind of theological formation which leads the teacher to greater moral and spiritual self-awareness and self-criticism. There is no concealing the fact that school RE constitutes a very severe personal exposure of a teacher. Lonergan's analysis of the discipline of dialectic explains, I believe, why this is so.

Fourthly, the actual practice of religious education in this country is in a remarkably confused state. The rise to political prominence of the phenomenological theory of RE has to be attributed to the dominance of a quite separate ideology, the ideology of libertarian-pluralism. The fact that this ideology is grossly intolerant of other social philosophies is irrelevant to the phenomenological theory in its true form. But I have little doubt that when libertarian-pluralism is eventually publicly discredited, the apparently unanswerable reasonableness of the phenomenological theory will vanish, and we will discover that it is undesirable to base a system of religious education upon a philosophical theory of religion. Religious education must be based on the beliefs and practices of actual religions, of which the best interpreters are educated and self-critical practitioners.

NOTES

1. 'Religion as a Discipline', *Universities Quarterly*, vol 16, no. 5, December 1962, pp. 48–53.

2. *Commitment and Neutrality in Religious Education*, Geoffrey Chapman 1979, pp. 90f.

3. J. S. Bezzant, *Objections to Christian Belief*, 1963, p. 89.

4. Edited by John Hick, SCM Press 1977.

5. See chapter 8, p. 130.

6. See Edward Hulmes, op. cit., p. 15.

7. Bernard Lonergan, *Method in Theology*, DLT 1972, p. 247.

8. Ibid., p. 253.

9. Dr Leslie Francis is Leverhulme Research Fellow, YMCA, London. See Farmington Occasional Paper No. 6, 'Christianity and the Child Today. A research perspective on the situation in school'.

10 Doctrine and Theology
Christopher Butler

The Education Act of 1944 remains the legal basis of schooling in what are called county schools. It did not directly affect independent schools, which were not under scrutiny at that time. It made provision for religious education as part of the formation to be given to children, and at that time it was taken for granted that religion in this country meant Christianity. It was of course recognized that there was a variety of Christian denominations. The ecumenical movement was already at work, though its effects were much less developed than today. Although the Church of England had a national priority over the other denominations, as being the established church of England, provision was made for the drawing up of agreed religious syllabuses which, it was hoped, would be acceptable to the several denominations.

There is a difficulty about agreed religious syllabuses. If separate churches each have their own official doctrine, and if this doctrine is in some respects at variance with that of other churches, there is a danger that an agreed syllabus will turn out to be a compromise document or 'reduction' of doctrine to a highest common factor. If you happen to believe that the doctrine of your church constitutes an organic whole,[1] this reductionism is unsatisfactory. One may suspect that so-called religious instruction, in consequence of the 1944 Act, tended to become scriptural exegesis rather than doctrinal information. The same problem arises, of course, in a much more acute form, when, as today, the classrooms of our schools are filled with a mixture not only of different forms of Christianity but of different religions: Jews, Moslems, Hindus, Sikhs, and so on. Is there not a tendency today to substitute for the old agreed syllabuses something which is hardly distinguishable from a watered-down and dangerously sketchy sort of 'comparative religion'? And as each religion has its own identity, will not this mean that so-called religious instruction will become not the presentation of the doctrinal content of a religion but a non-committal exercise in human history, the sort of thing that was offered to us a few years ago in a Television Series called 'The Long Search'.[2] I would on the whole prefer that schoolchildren were given the opportunity of rejecting a religion which they had been accurately and religiously taught at school, than left to drift around in a morass of half-baked history of man's uncontrolled sallies into the alleged unknown.

The Catholic Church stood rather aloof from all this. We had our own Catholic schools. Up to that date, the majority of these were parish schools of what were then called the elementary grade. In elementary schools children were taught from the age of five up to fourteen, the general school-leaving age. A minority of children might secure scholarships at grammar or other secondary schools; and some parents were able to afford to pay for the secondary education of some or all of their children. The Act of 1944 made secondary schooling available and free for all children, and the age of free entry was fixed at 11; this meant, of course, that the Catholic elementary schools lost their pupils at that age, instead of keeping them till they reached the age of fourteen. It thus presented the Catholic Church with a great challenge to provide itself with Catholic secondary schools on a large scale; hitherto the only provision for Catholic secondary schooling, apart from the expensive boarding schools, was a scattering of secondary (usually grammar) schools where fees had to be paid; these were often kept low, but at best the great majority of Catholic children received no formal secondary education. It became imperative, after the 1944 Act, to remedy this situation, since otherwise Catholic children, having reached the age of 11, would in most cases have had to continue their schooling in non-Catholic schools. The challenge was accepted and, at great expense to the Catholic population, the gap was filled. But the secondary schools were not parish schools, like the old elementary schools or, as they were now termed, the primary schools. In many cases arrangements were made for chaplains to secondary schools; but valuable as their work was, the loss of close links with the parish could not be remedied.

The Catholic schools of this country were not created by theologians, but by the Catholic people as a whole, under the direction of the bishops. Not unnaturally, bishops and people are concerned about the religious education offered in these schools, and their authority is indisputable. Similar considerations apply to the Catholic Colleges of Higher Education. At the same time, since a major part of the capital cost and the cost of running our schools is paid by civil authorities, the government, the local authorities, and indeed the English people at large have a right to a say in our schools; a right which is catered for, among other ways, by the statutory representaion of local government authority in the governing bodies of the schools.

So where does theology come into this picture? And what do I mean by theology?

One should distinguish theology from doctrine; and it may make this distinction clearer if we accept Lonergan's analysis of the three components which, taken together, give rise to human knowledge. These components are: experience, understanding, and judgment.[3] In the Christian religion experience includes the content of revelation in Christ. It is a lived experience, and presupposes that an individual is sharing in the life of the Christian community and is open to the tradition and ethos of that community. Theology, I suggest, is the activity of understanding that experience by a process of reflection upon it. Understanding cannot function in a vacuum, and it is experience which provides understanding with its raw material. But understanding is a stage in knowledge, not the perfection of knowledge, which comes with reflection, not only on experience but on understanding, and moves from understanding to reasonable affirmation.

If I am right in thinking that theology is the work and fruits of the understanding of religious experience, then theology is not a science which makes affirmations, but an intellectual process which offers hypotheses together with the grounds which underpin those hypotheses and make them more or less plausible.

In the Christian community, as distinct from the individual Christian person, affirmation is the task of the community itself, a task which is in part undertaken, in a representative fashion, by the official 'teaching authority' of the church (it will save misunderstanding if I am allowed to speak of doctrinal, rather than teaching, authority; since much of what we call teaching in schools is at the level of understanding rather than of affirmation). Since theology, as an exercise of understanding, depends upon the data that it proposes to understand, it is obvious that it cannot create its own data. If it is to be Christian theology, as distinct from the sociology of religion, comparative religion, and religious philosophy, it can only accept data provided by the church; and if it rejects such data or any intrinsic element in such data, it ceases to be Christian theology.

At this point it becomes necessary to consider more closely the way in which doctrinal authority operates in the church (I speak as a Roman Catholic). The church has a commission, received through Christ from God, to carry to mankind the gospel, the Good News, of salvation in Christ. It is enabled for this commission by the Holy Spirit who 'brings all things to its remembrance' of the message of Christ himself. That it will not fail in its proclamation of this message is assured by God himself in Christ: 'Behold, I am with you all the days to the end of the age.' The church's proclamation and teaching of its message is thus 'infallible' and the church herself is 'indefectible'.

When we say that the church's doctrine is infallible, what do we mean by the church? We mean the whole body of believers united in that 'communion', that fellowship and community, which relates each believer both with his fellow-believers and with God himself in and through Christ. There has been much talk about papal infallibility; but the pope only makes sense when seen as the voice of the whole church and therefore of every baptized person.

The church as a fellowship and community is not just a purely spiritual and incorporated mystical entity, known to God but only believed in by men. It has a visible, and therefore an institutional, aspect; in somewhat the same way as a nation has its constitution and government and a trade union has its officers and executive rules. Catholics believe that the church, in this its visible aspect, is represented at local level by the bishops, and at the universal level by the head of the episcopal 'college', the pope. It is helpful to see both the bishops and the pope, the chief bishop, as primarily organs of unity rather than as in the first instance organs of law or even of doctrine.

There are however times when, in the continuing dialogue between the church and the world and the dialogue between Christians themselves, it is judged necessary to clarify verbally a disputed question regarding the content of the gospel. It is not feasible to bring the whole church together for such an act of judgment. Catholics believe that bishops collectively have a particular role, emanating perhaps from their role as unifiers, to make such judgments on behalf of the whole People of God. Such judgments can in theory be made in an informal way; but in moments of real crisis it has on several occasions been thought prudent to gather the bishops together in 'ecumenical council'. The judgment of an ecumenical council on a disputed detail of the gospel can be of a definitive kind, both articulating the mind of the church at large and binding the faithful to what the judgment teaches. We believe that in such cases the church's own infallibility is exercised in and as the infallibility of the bishops in council.

Something similar can be said of the infallible teaching role of the pope. His 'irreformable' definitions are an expression of the infallibility of the church herself and more specifically of the bishops.

But very obviously, bishops, ecumenical councils and popes address themselves not only to the determination of irreformable judgments on the actual content of the gospel and on matters so genuinely entailed by the gospel that the one cannot be maintained without the other, but to matters of contingent concern and doctrinal determinations which are of a provisional and less than universal application. In this area the teaching of one's local bishop, of the 'college' of bishops, and of the pope is on the one hand official and on the other hand not irreformable, not binding on the fundamental Christian assent of the faithful.

What is the attitude of theology to the church's doctrine, to the teaching role of bishops and the pope, and to doctrinal judgments emanating from them? I note in passing that the response of theologians should not be viewed as comparable to the response of a soldier to orders given by his superior officers. Soldiers are required not to reason why but to do and die; and they are liable to sanctions of a merely human kind. Authority in the church is different. All genuinely Christian authority is a sort of sacramentalization of the authority of Christ and of God revealed in Christ. And divine authority is, to the extent that God is love, not an authority of command but an authority of appeal. The truly Christian response of theology to doctrinal authority is basically an act of love, an act motivated by and embodying love; an act, therefore, of responsible freedom – for only responsible freedom can actualize love.

This having been said, it is obvious that Christian theology accepts and operates within the context of the church's infallible doctrine. It would not be Christian theology if it failed to do so. What remains true is that every verbal formula which gives expression to a doctrinal judgment is subject to exegesis and hermeneusis. Lonergan maintains, and I agree, that truth resides not in verbal statements but in the judgment which such a statement seeks to express. A verbal statement is not true or false in itself; it is adequate or inadequate to a true or false judgment. A very obvious case is the doctrine that 'outside (or apart from) the church there is no salvation'. This doctrine has an august lineage: cf. Matt. 10.15, on the subject of those who reject the message of the twelve apostles: 'It shall be more tolerable on the day of judgment for the land of Sodom and Gomorrah than for that town.' The church cannot be expected to relativize such primordial Christian teaching. But one remembers Chesterton's observation that the church has spent its life seeking to make tolerable the intolerable quality of the original gospel; and the Church's own exegesis of the doctrine that there is no salvation apart from her is now so nuanced that a critic has argued that it amounts to a sheer contradiction of the traditional formula.

What, however, is there about doctrine that is official, as coming from one's bishop, from the college of bishops, or from the pope, but not irreformable?

Let us take a case. A theologian is working, or a teacher teaching, in the diocese of a bishop who is prone to doctrinal affirmations. Let us suppose that this bishop, in a pastoral instruction, has laid it down that the theory of evolution is a contradiction of revealed truth. What is the teacher or theologian to do? He is in a situation comparable to a 16-year-old whose father, pontificating at dinner, announces that Einsteinian relativity is 'all bunk', pernicious nonsense. I imagine that the dutiful and loving son is called upon, in such circumstances, to maintain and express his respect for his father. But if he 'knows better' than his father the real status of the Einsteinian theory, he is not required to accept his father's verdict as true; he might be well advised to divert the conversation to the iniquities of Sir Geoffrey Howe.

I think that the theologian or teacher is called upon to a similar combination of respect and non-assent when faced with his bishop's obscurantism. And I think the same is true when the doctrine in question has the wider and more august authority of the college of bishops and of the pope. Teachers and theologians in such circumstances have the arduous task of combining loyalty and respect for constituted authority with respect for the truth. A whole casuistry might be developed along these lines, but I forbear.

In all this I have been concerned about theology as subordinate to doctrine. But there is another side of the coin. The church and her official teachers (bishops and pope) are to a very large extent dependent upon and indebted to theology. After all, the reasonable judgment by which the human mind comes into possession of knowledge does not arise directly out of experience, even religious experience, but out of understanding based on experience. Bishops are not necessarily theologians any more than the mass of the faithful – while 'theologizing' in the broad sense of that term – are professional theologians. They are therefore under an obligation to listen to expert theology. It is perhaps true that in the more recent past neither bishops nor popes have acknowledged very noticeably their debt to contemporary theologians; but I suspect that they have in fact often made use of theological advice – not always the best theological advice available. The second Vatican Council was undoubtedly deeply indebted to theological advice and help from theologians, some of them among the best in the world of their day; and real attempts were made to ensure that the Council's doctrine did not run counter to the insights of good scholarship and deep reflection.

There is a remarkable difference between the status in the church of theologians on the one hand and bishops and the pope on the other. Bishops and popes hold offices and exercise functions that are bound up with the institutional structures of the church; and since we believe that God never places a man or woman in an office without giving him or her the help of the Holy Spirit for the due exercise of that office (what is called 'the grace of state') we do well to remember that these officials are guided by the Holy Spirit – at least in a negative sense that they will never use their function of 'infallible' teaching to mislead the church irreparably. There is no divine status or order of theologians in the church. Theological proficiency is, rather, a 'charism' in the narrow sense that that word is given in Vatican II and in common parlance today. Theology, in other words, is chronically unofficial, though this does not mean that it can be dispensed with or that it has no important role to play in the life of the church. On the contrary, the role of understanding religious experience is, as I have argued, indispensable if the church is to attain the knowledge of the faith. We are warned by St Paul not to 'quench' the Spirit. This means that bishops and Popes should respect theology, give its practitioners liberty to pursue their work, and listen to what they have to tell the officials.

The reflections offered in this paper are reflections of a Roman Catholic. In the Roman Catholic Church great emphasis has been laid on doctrine and on the vocation of bishops and popes to teach doctrine. The very Roman Catholic word 'magisterium', often today applied in a loose way to the church's episcopal and papal office-holders, really refers to their doctrinal role. This emphasis on contemporary doctrinal 'authority' may seem to be absent from some other form of Christianity, and I am not sure that my sharp distinction between theology and doctrine will sound familiar to, for example, Anglicans. In this connection, however, I should like to relate a true story from the experiences of the Anglican/Roman Catholic International Commission, or rather its forerunner, the Preparatory Commission. At one of our meetings there was an outburst from a Roman Catholic member, who said that it was impossible to discuss matters with Anglicans because they all held different beliefs. On that occasion an Anglican bishop was chairing the meeting. With some dignity, if not primness, he admitted that there was a freedom of discussion in the Church of England which might strike a Roman Catholic as strange. Nevertheless, the Church of England had its own doctrines; and these could be discovered *by examining her official formularies*. Implicitly, he was distinguishing between the exploratory nature of theology and the doctrinal authority of the church herself coming to expression in formularies which were usually of episcopal origin.

I suggest, however, that if the Roman Catholic Church is going to take Vatican II's ecclesiology seriously, she will have to recognize that, though she teaches that the church of Christ 'subsists' in the Roman Catholic communion, still the church *exists* outside the visible limits of that communion; and if the church so exists, then the witness of Christian theologians who are not Catholics needs to be taken a good deal more seriously by the Roman Catholic Church than was customary in times before Vatican II endorsed the ecumenical movement. In this connection, one may look hopefully not only to the coming publication of ARCIC's completed work but to the work and eventual publications of the Roman Catholic/Orthodox Commission recently established by the officialdom of those two great communions.

Perhaps a concluding observation will not be out of place. Every doctrinal formulation comes out of a particular cultural situation in which the church finds herself at any particular time. Officialdom as such is ill-equipped to distinguish cultural and therefore limited meanings from what Fr Chirico, in his book, *Infallibility*, calls universal meanings. It will always be the task of theology to draw attention to this distinction and to enable the church to understand it and draw the necessary inference.

NOTES

1. See Introduction, p. 2.
2. See chapter 4, p. 63.
3. See chapter 9, pp. 137f.

11 Theology and Ideology
John Macquarrie

Since the time of the Enlightenment, the West has been very much captivated by a certain ideal of knowledge. The adjectives 'objective' and 'value-free' have been used to describe this ideal of knowledge. These adjectives indicate that it is to be purified of all 'subjective' influences and that it is to stick to facts, disregarding any value-judgments upon them. This also implies an investigator who is 'detached' from and 'uninvolved' with the subject matter, an investigator who is a pure observer of phenomena. Indeed, if possible, it would be desirable to replace the human observer by some impersonal equipment. These requirements have led in course of time to the development of the empiricist theory of knowledge. From universally observable phenomena one is supposed to proceed by universally accepted logical methods of induction to universally accepted generalizations.

But this ideal has nowadays been more and more called into question. On the one hand, some philosophers of science have criticized the logic of induction, and have argued that imagination plays just as important a part in scientific discovery as does observation, and that in any case the scientist is never the passive recipient of objective data but is already selecting and evaluating the phenomena. Karl Popper boldly declares, 'There can be no pure observational language, since all languages are impregnated with theories and myths.'[1] On the other hand, a different group of philosophers have been arguing that all knowledge has an inescapable personal dimension. Into every act of knowing there enters, albeit tacitly, something of the interests and values of the knower. Michael Polanyi has been the best known exponent of this view in Britain. He goes so far as to say that 'any attempt rigorously to exclude our human perspective from our picture of the world must lead to absurdity'.[2]

The 'value-free' ideal itself implies a value-system, for which, in its own terms, it can offer no justification. If it has any plausibility at all, this would be only in the most formal and abstract subjects, such as mathematics and physics. This helps to explain why Descartes and his successors prized mathematics above all other sciences, and tried to assimilate all knowledge to the mathematical ideal. Spinoza tried to treat ethics by the methods of geometry, and nearer our own time Carnap envisaged in his concept of 'physicalism' the reduction of all sciences to the language of physics. Such attempts surely do merit the charge of absurdity. Today there would be much more sympathy than formerly for the belief that each science has its own appropriate methodology, and that in varying degrees the interests and values of the investigator will enter into his work. Even the mathematician derives satisfaction from the aesthetic elegance of his demonstrations.

Let us turn from these general considerations to the special question of religion and theology. Here we may note that the Oxford Theology Honour School, when founded in the nineteenth century, was designed to conform to the objective and value-free ideals that were influential at that time. This accounts for the heavily biblical and historical orientation of the school. One could hardly teach or examine anyone on the subjects of, say, God or the eucharist – that would be to stray into the realms of private subjective opinion,[3] so it was supposed. The attitude was reinforced by the acute denominational sensitivities prevailing in those days. But it was all right, let us say, to teach and examine Anselm's doctrine of God or Ratramnus' teaching about the eucharist. These are matters of ascertainable fact, and, at least in theory, they can be objectively taught and objectively examined. This traditional attitude helps to explain why England has been weak in systematic theology, but strong in historical theology.[4] A few years ago, a move was made to reduce the historical bias in the Oxford Honour School, and to allow more room to systematic theology. The move was defeated by a coalition of those who believe that, in order to be academically respectable, theology may deal only with the question of who said what, not with the substantive questions of religious truth themselves. When a much more modest change in the curriculum was introduced to replace the defeated scheme, I myself heard someone say in the discussion: 'You mustn't pry into a person's private beliefs!'

Of course, there is a difference between theology and religious belief. The difference is twofold. A religious belief has a measure of naïveté or immediacy about it. It is confessional language, evoked by some powerful impression made on the believer. Examples would be the confessions of the apostles Peter and Thomas recorded in the New

Testament expressing their reponse to Jesus of Nazareth. 'You are the Christ!' says Peter (Mark 8.29). 'My Lord and God,' says Thomas (John 20.28). Theology is a second order language,[5] and, therefore, more sophisticated, more critical and more reflective. The theologian might begin from confessions of faith, like the two quoted, but he then enquires about the meaning of the terms used, such as 'Christ' and 'Lord' and 'God', he enquires further about the implications of these terms, their coherence, the reasons that led to their being applied to Jesus, and so on. In this way he may come to develop a complete christology. The second element in the twofold difference concerns the mode of assent. If we may use Newman's terminology, a religious belief calls for real assent. Peter and Thomas were committing themselves to Jesus Christ in a fairly total way, and it was certainly more than an intellectual act. They were taking up an existential stance. But when one begins to theologize, reflectively and critically, one has, so to speak, taken a step back. Sometimes, of course, a theological belief may be passionately held. One can readily suppose, for instance, that in eucharistic controversies, some have given real assent to such difficult doctrines as transubstantiation and consubstantiation. However, one may also suppose that a real assent could be given to the religious belief, in this case, in a real presence of Christ, but only a notional or even a modified assent to the theological interpretation.

If one accepts that there is the twofold difference just described between religious belief and theology, then this throws some light on the question whether someone who is not a believer could either study or teach theology. It seems to me that one could neither teach a subject nor study it with any seriousness unless one believed that it had some integrity and value. Thus, if someone supposed that the subject-matter of theology is non-existent or illusory, he could hardly be a serious student of theology or a teacher of theology. He might, of course, be a good student of philosophy or religion, trying to present a theory of religion as illusion, though I think some philosophers of religion would question this. But I would say that an atheist could not be a serious student or teacher of Christian theology. On the other hand, I would hesitate to say the same about an agnostic. An agnostic is unable to give real assent to first order religious beliefs, but he might have sufficient sympathy with them to take seriously the interpretation of these beliefs as found in the second order language of theology, and to teach theology effectively and conscientiously as a serious subject.[6]

I have criticized the notion of a detached or value-free study of religion and theology, and claimed that some minimal sympathy must be present. This does not mean for one moment, however, that the only alternative to the value-free approach is some form of subjectivism or propaganda. In modern totalitarian states, the sociopolitical ideology of such a state or even a complete philosophy of life is propagated with all the resources of the educational system and the various media. Perhaps religion could be propagated in such a way also, and no doubt it has sometimes been so propagated. But, certainly from the Christian point of view, such a propagation of religion would be self defeating. For Christianity has as one of its basic teachings respect for the human person,[7] and this kind of propaganda is a manifest disregard for the person, who is seen as an object to be manipulated. Equally, such an activity is an offence against any educational theory that respects personal integrity.

Leaving aside the question of propaganda, it is even doubtful if Christian teaching should take the form of apologetics, that is to say, a form in which it is presented as superior to alternative beliefs. If this were to be done without falling into mere propaganda, then one would need to be very careful to state clearly and give a fair hearing to the alternative viewpoints and their objections to Christian belief. So often the apologist presents the alternatives in some weak or implausible form, so that one suspects he is setting up a straw man with the sole purpose of demolishing it. Karl Popper truly remarks that 'there is no point in discussing or criticizing a theory unless we try all the time to put it in its strongest form, and to argue against it only in that form'.[8] A common error is to present some generalized argument and then to show its weakness. But I think one has got to be concrete, and face the actual objections and criticisms of major atheistic thinkers, such as Feuerbach, Marx, Nietzsche, Freud, Sartre and others.

But even if one seeks to be as fair as possible in such an apologetic presentation of Christianity, some theologians would still believe that a controversial statement of this kind is unsatisfactory. They would say that the best defence of Christian faith is simply to say what it is, to let it be seen in its own light, so to speak, without engaging in polemics. Apologetic arguments for the reasonableness or superiority of Christian belief have their place only or chiefly when doubts and questions arise, either in our own minds or in the minds of those whom we are addressing.

I have mentioned socio-political philosophies that are sometimes propagated into totalitarian states, and what I had in mind were, for instance, Fascism, Nazism, Marxism, Maoism and the like. These have become substitute religions in our time, and they are believed and preached with all the fervour of a religious fanatic. They are sometimes called 'ideologies'. Actually, this word 'ideology' has several meanings, and I do not believe that this one is the most important. In any case, we have seen that Christianity could not become an ideology in this sense without self-contradiction. It would be a bogus form of Christianity that sought to propagate itself with all the modern techniques of persuasion without any respect for the reason and conscience of the persons concerned.

The word 'ideology' has become nowadays a term of reproach. It is surely an irony that when we hear it, we associate it with some totalitarian socio-political doctrine, more likely than not with Marxism. This is an irony because Marx too used this term as one of reproach or even abuse, but presumably he did not dream that it would be applied to his own theories. In 1846, along with Engels, he wrote a work called *German Ideology*. Here the word is used in its distinctively Marxist sense to mean the beliefs and theories that are produced by the economic conditions of society. Marx believed that philosophies which claim to be products of pure reason are in fact expressions of class interest. If one carried this view to extreme lengths, obviously it would lead to a self-destroying scepticism. Yet we can have little doubt that, as against the Enlightenment glorification of reason, Marx was correct in claiming that interest enters into all our thinking. 'Ideology', in this sense, is something subtler and more important than ideology in the popular sense of a consciously propagated socio-political philosophy. In this other, Marxist, sense, ideology is an unconscious distortion of thought, derived from the influence of class interests. Marx believed himself that only the proletariat is free of ideology and has a clear vision of things as they really are, and so he sought to escape from the slide into scepticism.

Marx's own view of ideology has been criticized at many points, especially his attempt to derive it solely from economic class interest, and to exempt one class from its influence. But the residual truth in his view has been developed by later philosophers of neo-Marxist tendency, especially by Habermas in his book *Knowledge and Interest*. He broadens the range of the idea of interest to include more than economic factors, criticizes Kant and other philosophers who have believed that one can aspire to a wholly rational understanding of the world, but avoids a thoroughgoing scepticism by holding that through self-reflection and self-criticism we can overcome the worse effects of the interest which inevitably enters into our knowledge. Rather similar views are to be found in another neo-Marxist, Marcuse. He argues that even science and technology are by no means neutral or value-free. They are already impregnated with a consumption-oriented value system which is hostile to the development of a free society. But he also believes that these false values can be overcome by critical reason.

It seems to me that one of the major challenges to theology today and to its teachers is to face the question of the relation of theology to ideology, in the sense in which this latter term is used by Marxist and neo-Marxists. We have seen that Christian theology is not, and cannot be, an ideology in the popular sense of the term – at least, if it ever became such, it would have destroyed itself. But is there perhaps an admixture of ideology in theology, in the more subtle Marxist sense of the term? Is it possible indeed to avoid it? Let me give a very simple example. For centuries the clergy of the Church of England were recruited almost exclusively from the two ancient universities of Oxford and Cambridge, with their upper-class backgrounds. Was it not inevitable that this should have affected, even if unconsciously, their way of presenting Christianity, causing them to emphasize those elements which agree with their interests, and to play down other elements that were less comfortable? Could this explain in part the alienation of the industrial masses from the church? Does it not also explain in part the Oxford Honour School of theology, for that supposedly objective and value-free study of theology itself reflects a very definite scheme of values, that of the leisured intellectual?

It seems to me further that the challenge of ideology is making itself felt very sharply in the theological world today. For centuries, Christian theology was the almost exclusive preserve of a well-defined segment of the human race. Theologians were Europeans, and later North Americans; they worked in universities and were steeped in the traditions of Western, especially classical, learning; they were of middle-class or upper-class background; they were almost entirely of the male sex. Can it be seriously denied that this long association of theology with this segment of society has led to the infiltration into theology of ideas and values that derive from this social and cultural background, and have no basis in Christianity itself?[9] While, conversely, other elements in the Christian message may have been unconsciously suppressed? At any rate, we seem to have come to a crisis, when hitherto silent and inarticulate groups are demanding that they too should have a share in shaping theology.

Let me mention four such groups.

In India, China, Africa and the Caribbean, there is a demand for what has become known as indigenous theology, that is to say, theology expressed in the images and concepts current in these cultures, in place of what to them are the alien concepts and images of the West. Indigenous theology was one of the leading items on the agenda of the worldwide Anglican Consultative Council of 1976, and already much has been achieved in both theology and liturgy in the matter of breaking out of Western moulds and using indigenous resources.

In the United States, although the black section of the population has always been profoundly religious, it has had until recently very little influence in theology or in the ethos of the mainline denominations. But now black theology has made its appearance, a type of theology which tries to understand Christianity in terms of the black experience. For this theology, Christ is black – not literally, for no one knows what his complexion was, but in the important sense that he is identified with the black experience.

In South America, where ever since independence was gained from the former Spanish and Portuguese rulers, there has been in most of the republics an almost unbroken series of tyrannous regimes, whether of the right or the left, now we hear of 'liberation theology', a theology which is conceived in terms of the concrete situation of these nations. For them, abstract Oxbridge debates on 'the myth of God incarnate' would be a meaningless and irrelevant exercise in theology. They are interested in what Christianity has to say about social justice and the liberation of the oppressed.

The last group I want to mention is not a minority group, like those already cited, but half the human race, namely, women. Though women have been active in the church from the beginning, and have provided their fair share of saints, martyrs and mystics, they have until recently been virtually excluded from theology. Is there not at least a strong probability that the monarchical, masculine, dominating concept of God, against which many people have rebelled in modern times, has been in part due to the male monopoly of theology, and the unconscious interests and prejudices which thus found their way into theology? Certainly, many of the new breed of women theologians believe that this has been the case, and are determined to let a different way of expressing matters be heard.

But will not this proliferation of different theologies, each seeing things from a distinctive viewpoint, each penetrated by special interests and a special ideology, have an utterly fragmenting effect, so that Christian theology will disappear in a mass of partial and often distorted points of view? I do not think so. There never will be one all-embracing theology, expressing in proper proportions all the truths of Christian faith. Certainly, our traditional Western theologies could not claim to have done that. They too were infected by ideology, just as much as black theology or liberation theology, though we were for the most part unaware of it and perhaps thought that Thomas Aquinas or Luther or Calvin was the universal voice of Christianity. But to deny that there will ever be an adequate all-embracing theology is not to resign oneself to sheer fragmentation or pluralism. Certainly, value-free theology is a chimera. No theology is free from ideological value-judgments. But a global theology is still possible, and is indeed a necessity for our shrinking world. I mean, a theology that would honestly admit the legitimacy of different interests and would encourage their expression. It would not try to harmonize them all in one inclusive statement, but would let them correct and enrich one another.

To sum up: theology, like other intellectual disciplines, is never value-free. To some extent, it will always embody the interests and valuations of the theologian. It is therefore never free from ideology, but the distorting effects of ideology can be minimized by encouraging the theologians to work from different social and cultural backgrounds, to become as far as possible aware of these and critical of them, and to allow their findings to correct each other dialectically.

NOTES

1. Karl Popper, *Objective Knowledge*, OUP 1972, p. 146.
2. Michael Polanyi, *Personal Knowledge*, Routledge, ²1962, p. 1.
3. Edward Hulmes, *Commitment and Neutrality in Religious Education*, Geoffrey Chapman 1979, p. 15.
4. See chapter 9, pp. 140f.
5. See chapter 8, p. 123.
6. See chapter 6, p. 98.
7. See chapter 4, p. 70.
8. Popper, op. cit., p. 266.
9. See chapter 1, p. 31.

12 Understanding and Experience
Kenneth Wilson

'No one *can* speak the truth; if he has still not mastered himself. He *cannot* speak it; – but not because he is not clever enough yet.

'The truth can be spoken by someone who is already *at home* in it; not by someone who still lives in falsehood and reaches out from falsehood to truth on just one occasion' (L. Wittgenstein, *Culture and Value*, Blackwell 1980, p. 16e).

'A teacher may get good, even astounding, results from his pupils while he is teaching them and yet not be a good teacher; because it may be that, while his pupils are directly under his influence, he raises them to a height which is not natural to them, without fostering their own capacities for work at this level, so that they immediately decline again as soon as the teacher leaves the classroom. Perhaps this is how it is with me; I have sometimes thought so. (When Mahler himself conducted his students in training sessions he obtained excellent performances; the orchestra seemed to deteriorate at once when he was not conducting it himself) (ibid., p. 38e).

'I think the way people are educated nowadays tends to diminish their capacity for suffering. At present a school is reckoned good "if the children have a good time". And that used not to be the criterion. Parents moreover want their children to grow up like themselves (only more so), but nevertheless subject them to an education *quite* different from their own. Endurance of suffering isn't rated highly because there is supposed not to be any suffering – really it's out of date' (ibid., p. 71e).

'Anything your reader can do for himself leave to him' (ibid., p. 77e).

Introduction

One of the arts of teaching is that one enables the pupil to learn with
the absolute minimum of unlearning; that is that one takes the trouble
to make sure that one is not knowingly building on mistaken assumptions
which have to be corrected at a later stage of education. So, for example,
in teaching history one tries not only to encourage an appropriate
understanding of what constitutes evidence and how to use it, but also
to avoid a simplistic approach to the idea that the causes can easily be
identified, listed and remembered by rote. It is important to take this
into account from the earliest age.

   Now it is difficult enough to construct curricula in any discipline,
bearing in mind this criterion; in religion it is particularly hard because
of a special feature of religious studies. For whereas most disciplines
have an apparent immediate relevance, to the world of the child (yes,
even history!), religion is peculiarly an adult activity and lacks this
immediate relevance; it concerns the feelings, ideas and attitudes of
adults rather than of children, or even of adolescents. The myths,
stories, theories, and practices that go to make up the life of a religion
are the result of adult reflection and enquiry in the light of adult
experience. The consequence is that in teaching such things to children,
if one is not extremely careful, one is not so much dealing with an
expression of their own present human experience, as with doctrines,
events and narratives which acquire some apparently objective reality
through being secondhand and having to be learned. And this totally
changes the possible understanding of religion open to the pupil. Instead
of a dynamic relationship between the expression of religious faith and
the individual's human experience it is fixed, and the pupil lacks the
linguistic dexterity to develop each in the light of the other. The unreality
of religion is assured. With such a gap in the relation between the
material of religious faith and human experience the pupil finds
continuous mature reflection more difficult. The problem of course has
been exacerbated by the secularization of society. For it is now so rarely
the case that the family by conversation and the practice of the faith,
both public and private, provides the ground for the talking out and
exploration of the meaning of what is being learned. So what do we do?
The proposal here is that we take with greater seriousness the study of
theology, and from that take criteria which are not simply relevant to
the teaching of religion but to education and the curriculum as a whole.
In this essay discussion concerns the 16+ group, but clearly the
perspective should pervade the whole of our approach to religious
education. But first attention must be given to theology itself.

1. What is it to theologize?

To theologize is to enquire. Such a simple statement glosses over many difficulties and perplexities, but it above all distinguishes it as an activity, and opposes it to the mere reporting of information and the passing on of fixed ideas. It is an enquiry based upon the assumption that it makes sense to ask about meaning and purpose in human life. This assumption is by no means a trivial one since whether it does make sense to talk of the meaning of life has been the subject of much discussion, especially within philosophy. However, it is because theology makes the assumption that it makes sense to talk about meaning in life that it is concerned with what meaning can be given to the question of whether there is a God. Christian theology is a special case of theological enquiry, and claims that there is positive illumination for the human spirit when it concerns itself with the question of God as a personal being. This is partly because it is involvement with such central questions that allows one to discuss with honesty and conviction the implications of atheism. At this stage not just what meaning life has, but whether life has any meaning becomes paradoxically a living pre-occupation of faith. One might even say that to theologize is to concern oneself with the question, 'has life any meaning'?

To deal with such a question is indeed a matter of the self and its capacity to enquire, not simply a matter of objective enquiry, for it is of the essence of theologizing that one recognizes that the enquiry affects the person who is enquiring. The astronomer who wishes to analyse the red-shift in the movement of a star is not involved with the results of his enquiry in the same way as the same person would be if he or she were enquiring about the nature of human love or whether there was truth in the claim that the world was better thought of as a creation or simply as a universe. This is because to think honestly in the latter contexts requires honesty with oneself, not just a public honesty. To think thoughts that one would rather not think, with all the consequences for personal and social life which one would rather not entertain, is so hard that we have learned to recognize a temptation to self-deception as a crucial ingredient to be borne in mind, when assessing our own and other's statements about meaning and purpose in life. It is thus a significant matter that the study of theology is usually accompanied by attention to spirituality, for spirituality involves those disciplines and practices which encourage and develop honest thinking. Spirituality is a set of practices which enable the student to cope with the growing awareness of what it is to be a person who enquires, and who must enquire in order to be.

And one might emphasize the point by claiming that it is precisely engagement with the question of meaning through theologizing which brings the possibility of full personal maturity. It is grappling with the issues thus raised, encouraged by the wisdom found in the traditions of spirituality, that will bring a person to know himself and his world with clarity and sense.

But in order to have a chance of doing this one has to be able to talk, to be in possession of the languages which enable one both to express what one wants to say, and to enquire accurately and responsibly about one's experience. The range of uses here must be very large, but language will be employed to describe accurately, to question the implied limits of experience, and to reflect upon the meaning and significance of experience. And because language is itself acquired in a social context we are necessarily talking of communication, of using language with others in such a way as to learn from and respect a different experience rather than simply to persuade others to accept our own perspective. Language is no panacea, for it may both delimit possible experience, and enable us to question it; it both makes communication possible with others and can destroy the basis of it. The art is to use language in order to enable one to grow in love of the object of one's enquiry and thus accept one's relationship with it.

For Christian theology the meaning of life is bound up with enquiry about the nature of God, and the purpose of that enquiry is to enable one to grow in love of him and the service of his purposes in the world. The use of language in Christian theologizing is bent to this end.

If we are to approach the teaching of religion, therefore, from the point of view of theology, the fundamental point to bear in mind is that it is a crucial form of human and humanizing enquiry about the meaning of life. Since questions about the meaning of life are adult matters, it is clear that there are problems for the creation of a curriculum which would be immediately relevant to children which would not be misleading as an introduction to theologizing. Furthermore, the curriculum as a whole may lack contexts in which children learn to reflect in such a way as to make possible such enquiring; spirituality and the curriculum do not obviously go together. Yet without personal support, and the self-awareness which stems from it there will always be a tendency to reduce enquiry to the cataloguing of other people's enquiries. Such a conclusion would be, of course, not only the death of religious education, but the death of education. Perhaps education as a whole needs the unique ingredient of religious education understood from a theological perspective, if it is to encourage human flourishing rather than the mere repetition of experience. Radical questioning of the meaning and purpose of human life depends upon a radical approach to religious education.

2. *The passionate detachment of genuine enquiry*

One might call the approach which I am advocating one of passionate detachment. That is, that in order to enquire as a human being, one is committed to accepting in one's life the consequences of one's best, most objective knowledge. And the acceptance of the best objective knowledge is likely to cause suffering. That suffering might be because of what one is led consequently to believe about human nature, or about another human being, or about oneself. To accept limitations which one had not recognized, or to have to face the fact that there were false boundaries which one had set for oneself can be very hard; to accept such discoveries creatively requires grace and humility which are rare. Hence forms of enquiry, or systems of thought which domesticate the human spirit, and which appear to justify a restricted human environment, tend to flourish at the expense of those which bring limitations into question. So, for example, within theological enquiry, a systematic theology should be seen as a mode of enquiry, a thought experiment, not something to which one is committed, and which one therefore wishes to preserve at all costs. A style of painting, a tradition of literary construction, a pattern of scientific reflection, all come within the same category. The human being is free to think about what he is thinking, he is not necessarily limited to what he is thinking. But the attraction of defending a position is that it gives security, albeit a security which is inappropriate to true human flourishing. So that learning to listen to what others say, taking into account a wholly new perspective, responding to the results of enquiry in a new and developing discipline, are all part of the raw material of a religious education, if one takes theology seriously.

That it is important to learn how to give attention to traditions of reflection and approaches to problems which one does not share oneself is not to accept the necessity of relativism; rather the contrary. Only if one is convinced that it is worth searching for something in life is one going to pay attention to the ways in which others approach such questions; truth rather than taste is the ultimate concern.

This raises particular problems for the religious education of the adolescent, and most particularly for the 16+ period since experiment, taste, and passionate commitment rather than passionate detachment are likely to characterize the approach. Careful attention to the balance between passion and detachment will be necessary. In this regard an awareness of the personal process which enables theologizing to contribute to personal maturity will concentrate attention on the relationship between the acquisition of the best and most reliable objective information (detachment), and the personal questioning which enables it to be integrated into an outlook on life which is wholly acceptable to the pupil (suffering). Thus religious education is concerned with every aspect of the curriculum, history, geography, science, music, etc., as well as with the study of the questions of meaning which rise from them, and the religious traditions which incorporate living examples of how communities of faith have and are at present putting together these converging or disparate experiences. To the extent that religious studies has tried to remove the personal questions by objectifying the phenomena of religious experience it has made theological enquiry and therefore personal maturity more difficult: to the extent that it has translated religious experience into individual taste it has denied the seriousness of the community's search for meaning. The only way forward is to take with equal seriousness the objectivity of the enquiry about human experience, in so far as it is achievable, the personal questions as they arise, and the traditions which have worked for centuries to bring them together in fruitful dialogue, in order to see which of them is possible and worth continuing now. To introduce pupils to this dialogue is the abiding purpose of religious education.

In the light of this some general criteria may be offered for any curriculum in religious education. First, does it introduce pupils to theological enquiry? This will not be done simply by transmitting the thoughts that various traditions of reflection have had about God. It requires attention to methodology, to the ways in which an understanding of God has emerged in the light of experience. And the processes by which we make sense of our world are dynamic and interactive, for ideas about God lead to expectations about the way the world is, and actual experience of the world leads us to reshape and develop our understanding of God. For Judaism questions about the nature of God and his relationship to the world are raised by history, by, for example, the Exodus and the Exile and the Holocaust, and for the individual Jew by his or her regular recognition of the fact that despite all theory to support the view that the good would be blessed, those who were obedient to the tradition did not and do not necessarily prosper. For Christianity, the emergence of scientific enquiry gave rise to questions which changed the ways in which God's activity in the world could be understood. What the ways are in which the understanding of God was developed, or is being developed, are themselves interesting. How did the thought that God was a universal and not just a national God come to seem sensible within Judaism? What are the ideas which attract

Christian theologians as illuminating for the way in which they interpret and respond to the growing understanding of the natural world through science? Why those ideas and not others?

So the second criterion must concern the accuracy and the breadth of the knowledge which is essential if fruitful theological reflection is to take place. The curriculum of religious studies has a vested interest in the pattern of the whole curriculum, and in the structure of the curriculum within a particular discipline. Indeed without an awareness of what is taking place elsewhere in the pupil's learning experience, it will be difficult to introduce an appropriate experience of theological enquiry. Two particular issues affect therefore the teaching of religious studies in the 16+ period, the fact that all pupils have such a restricted and specialized area of study, and that religious education in so far as it takes place at all will find that place alongside general studies rather than arising out of the specialized areas of study. These features of the sixth form mean that it is easier to reduce religion to a matter of personal taste, or to social and ethical questions, than it is to see it as theological enquiry. Religious studies courses in the sixth form are too often constructed without knowledge of what is taking place elsewhere in the curriculum, and with simple reference to personal issues rather than to public questions of meaning and truth.

Knowledge of traditions of theological enquiry, and accurate, growing awareness of the natural world are not sufficient, for the purpose is to enable pupils to begin to think theologically, not simply to know how others have thought or now think. Thus a third criterion will concern the encouragement of the pupil in making sense of his own world and continuing the conversation he finds in the traditions for himself. And this implies a relationship between the teacher and the pupil, and a style of teaching which makes such encouragement plain. It is important to understand that such encouragement to personal enquiry does not imply the approval of an idea simply because a pupil has thought of it; on the contrary, it is to recognize that the purpose of religious education is to get people launched on the personal task of theological enquiry, and theological enquiry is not itself without criteria of truth and meaningfulness.

3. The education of a teacher

The teacher of such a subject needs special qualities and faces particular difficulties. It will of course be necessary to have clear knowledge of at least some of the traditions of theological enquiry. After all, in teaching mathematics one would not think it sensible to be blind to algebra or statistics. One would hope that the teacher would be able to draw on concepts and techniques from the wide range of traditions of reflection within mathematics in order to stimulate the freedom and the imagination of the pupil's response to a problem. And within any given subject area of mathematics one might have to play around with an expression for some time before one finally recognized it as one which could be tackled in a familiar way. The teacher of religious studies is wanting to encourage the same freedom, the same openness, the same sense of imaginative exploration with the problems that arise in making sense of one's experience theologically.

For example, with what presuppositions, and with what success has the problem of evil been tackled? To refer to the 'problem of evil' is to do no more than produce a mysterious expression within mathematics; one has to play around with it in order to put it into a form which one recognizes; one has to explore the question. And accordingly the question takes various shapes, and receives diverse if perhaps related answers in the various traditions to which one might attend.

To do this effectively a teacher requires as it were the freedom of the house, and needs to make it clear that this is what the pupil is invited to share. Christianity is not itself a single tradition of reflection though it has a certain coherence. The teacher needs to be free to draw on the vast resources of that tradition in order to stimulate and inform the enquiry of the pupil about meaning and purpose. Quite clearly also, an awareness of traditions of reflection other than the Christian will be important, and here the Marxist, the Muslim, and the Jewish have particular relevance. The catholicity of approach is necessary to the intellectual integrity of what is being attempted, and it is this which makes it impossible for religious education to be evangelical. It is not concerned to convert, but to introduce pupils to the conversations and issues which will enable them to enquire theologically for themselves.

However, even to have information at one's fingertips, to be immensely informed about the traditions of enquiry, even to know what to say in response to every pupil's enquiry is not sufficient, for if the teacher is to introduce pupils to theological enquiry, he or she needs to be enquiring. To the pupil the teacher who has arrived, and seems to know what is to be thought on every topic, has not actually begun to think. Furthermore, if the assumption of this paper is true, that to think theologically is a continuously necessary ingredient for personal growth to maturity, then the teacher who has ceased to enquire has ceased to grow. This is only to put into the life of the teacher of religious education the same necessity as pertains to every teacher; the teacher who has ceased to learn has ceased to be a teacher, though of course, he or she may be a means by which information is conveyed. Since, however, the conveying of information may well be done more efficiently in other ways, it is being a teacher which is crucial to the role of a teacher: no machine can be a teacher though it may teach.

The possession of knowledge of traditions of enquiry, the freedom of access to it and the ability to communicate them, all have their life for the pupil in the fact that the teacher is enquiring. In order to be enquiring in this sense, knowledge of the traditions of theological enquiry means also knowledge of the sorts of experiences which have encouraged people to think about and develop their ideas on meaning and purpose. A strict attention to religion may imply for some a concentration on a special category of experience called 'religious', and suggests attention to those experiences which have involved conversion or mediated a sense of God's presence. However, when one has widened one's horizon to theological enquiry then it has to be recognized that many varieties of experience have given rise to questions of meaning and purpose. Indeed far from it being the case that there is a special experience which begins theological reflection, for a particular individual, or a particular tradition it may be almost any experience. The beauty of mathematics, the sheer surprise that abstract thought can enable one to understand and predict events in the real world, the excitement of sport, the mystery of death, the vision of a piece of music, falling in love, a sense of failure, the destruction of a nation state, an overpowering sense of the presence of God, a delight in the grace of Jesus, the impression of power and love in Muhammed's response to God, the reading of a book, a sense of injustice, any one of these, and a thousand others has begun the search for meaning, the attempt to make sense of experience. The fact that they still do will make the wise teacher suspicious of all attempts to delimit and define what are to count as the 'correct' beginnings.

Further, it is only by remaining aware of the significance of other disciplines that the question will remain alive. Just as the stimulus to find meaning may come accidentally from almost any source, so also criticism and development of the process of theological enquiry may come from almost any source. Genetics may question the freedom of man, geology and palaeontology may question particular understandings of man's origins, psychology, sociology and history may illustrate and explain the devious uses to which a religious faith can be put, political and social concern may appear to make theological enquiry irrelevant, personal experience may make thinking about meaning and purpose almost impossible. But for these reasons, an extensive interest in other disciplines, combined with sufficient knowledge to be able to relate them in principle to the search for meaning is essential for the teacher. One might indeed say that apart from such an interest, the theological enquiry of the teacher will become increasingly private: however real it is for him it will be irrelevant to the needs, interests and perplexities of the pupil.

In order to engage with the pupil appropriately, yet one further quality is essential: the willingness to allow one's ideas to be exposed and plundered without fear, anxiety or resentment. And this is not such an easy matter. It is one thing to have information and ideas in which one wishes to interest others when those ideas can be presented with relative objectivity; it is quite another to be engaged in an enquiry for oneself, and therefore to have not only one's ideas, but in principle also oneself evaluated. Hence any course which purports to educate a teacher of religious education must take account of the need for the sort of personal growth which will enable such exposure to be tolerated with charity and interest. This will not only be a matter of the course itself, and the quality of relationships between students and staff, but also of the style of teaching and the level of communication between students themselves. For example, it would be misleading if the sole means of education was the lecture, if insufficient time was given to encouraging students to trust their own nose and follow their own enquiries, and if no recognition was made of the importance of the total life and ambience of the community, not only to the academic maturity, but also to the personal competence and therefore the professional efficiency of the potential teacher. If the teacher is to have any chance of encouraging that passionate detachment which best characterizes the nature of theological enquiry, he or she must acquire it, since it is a *sine qua non* for the task of allowing pupils the freedom to think for themselves, and to do so with critical acumen.

Such aims for religious education, and for the teacher of religious education may seem outrageously optimistic, and wide. After all, the word 'theological' has itself an air of irrelevance, and may be used by any politician to refer to an unrealistic approach to a problem. Not withstanding any truth there may be in some comments made on some approaches to the subject, nothing could be more important than the recognition that meaning and purpose in life are not private constructions without public implications or mere matters of personal taste. They affect the way people live, they may limit or enhance a person's understanding in life; they may result in the loss of opportunity to large parts of the world if they are not taken seriously. To equip students to deal with them sensitively and with a strict regard for truth and love would be a major contribution towards the enlargement of the opportunities that are open to man in the future. The expectations which are thus aroused of the teacher are, it may be said, too idealistic to be sensible.

But again, it seems that nothing is required but the best; indeed, perhaps nothing but the best is even useful.

Institutions, courses, teams of teachers will have to work on the implications in the way that best suits them. At Westminster College, the setting of education courses in a theological context, where upwards of 125 students per year either take religious studies as a main subject of their B.Ed., read for a degree in theology, or are now engaged in professional courses, having taken these subjects, makes it a particularly interesting place in which to experiment. The fact that over 80% of the students are resident, and that, therefore, there is enormous opportunity to talk out issues amongst both students and staff, is a most important dimension of the personal education which informs and provides the context for theological enquiry. The fact that courses may involve both students on initial training courses and teachers on in-service courses enhances the range of concern and expertise that is brought to bear. No student in this environment can avoid contact and conversation with theological enquiry. Meaning and purpose in life, not simply knowledge nor vocational task, should be a fundamental concern of education; religious education has a vital role to play both in the integration of the curriculum to make this obvious, and in the personal education of each pupil to make it a reality. The education of the potential teacher must be directed towards making this possible.

Theological conclusion

We call the world a creation and not a universe. By so doing we indicate that in some sense or another God is responsible for it. Yet it is a creation which is incomplete, for its purpose is to enable persons to flourish and not even God can by himself make persons. So the fulfilment of God's purpose in creating requires the fullest possible co-operation between God who is personal being, and that expression of the world's total being which can be personal, namely humanity. That co-operation is necessary to the full maturity of humanity too. For him it must involve both understanding the natural world (which must be taken to include humanity itself in all its aspects, scientific, social and personal), and the understanding of God. It is the putting together of these things in a continuous process of affectionate, responsive reflection that makes for human maturity, and which is the ultimate concern of religious education. By engaging in this activity a person discovers not only himself, but a God who is not absent but present, a God who is wholly committed himself to the fulfilment of his purpose in creating the world.

Unlike man, therefore, who frequently finds the pain of communication and the burden of personal exposure too great to tolerate, God is willing to be completely known, both in the manner of his creating, and in his own personal being. The celebration of this encourages man to continue or to begin again what he would otherwise be inclined to abandon, the task of making sense of his world. This cannot be an individual task for knowledge, language, truth, justice, peace, happiness, to name but a few of the essential things humans seek, are only genuinely available to each person to the extent that they characterize a community's life.

To place education in general and religious education in particular in such a context, with a full appreciation of the variety of traditions in which meaning and truth have been pursued, and with awareness of the need to identify and refine criteria of truth and meaningfulness, is the most crucial task of all who have responsibility for education. It was never more so than at the present time, when non-educational criteria seem to so many to be so much more central. Whether sufficient teachers of sufficient calibre and enthusiasm can be found, and sufficient staff to inspire them, remains the crucial question for our education service.

An Appraisal

Brenda Watson

What is impressive about this collection of papers on the growing-edge of education and of theology is the diversity of its contributors, in background and approach, combined with an awareness and real concern for genuine education. Very different religious commitments are reflected here, as well as the needs of schools as distinct as an inner city state comprehensive and a well-endowed monastic school. The measure of agreement is therefore noteworthy, and constitutes a significant argument for the teaching of theology at 16+.

Many valuable suggestions are made as to the way in which the subject should be approached in the classroom: Some of the points which seem to emerge a number of times are as follows:

1. Theology is intrinsically linked to what it means to be religious: it is not the prerogative of a highly specialized, privileged or intelligent group of people, but something which everyone who engages in any reflection about religion is already doing and needs to be helped to do well.

2. Theology should be seen as a living dialogue with experience, in which the vocabulary and insights of the past become available for making sense of what is happening personally and communally today.

3. Theology forms a continuum with all other aspects of human knowledge: it is not out on a limb, isolated and strange. It should be seen therefore as an integral part of the total school curriculum.

4. The teaching of theology must take account of the context in which it is taught – the ethos of the school, the attitudes and home environment of the pupils, etc. Uniformity in method and content is undesirable, for the way in which the subject is handled by the teacher needs to vary according to the needs and opportunities of different situations.

5. Theology is never static or stagnant: it develops and seeks new

forms of expression in changing cultural and historical settings and in relation to fresh understanding in other areas of human enquiry.

6. Theology should embrace some awareness not only of Jewish and Christian thought but also of that of other world religions, because this is the global context for the subject.

7. Theology should be taught in a way which clearly requires of the pupil rigorous thinking: it should not be seen as a soft option in which opinions do not have to be supported by reasons and evidence.

8. Theology is a highly controversial subject of enquiry: teacher and taught should therefore share in the search for ever greater illuminations, and the casting off of prejudice and misunderstandings.

9. Theology must be taught in an open, non-dogmatic manner which challenges pupils to think for themselves and not to accept anything just on the authority of teachers, parents or church.

10. Theology requires the creative use of the imagination as well as of logical powers of reasoning: starting-points and inferences have to be intuitively apprehended.

11. Theology deals with mystery understood in the profoundest sense of that term: it therefore calls for qualities of humility, reticence and the ability to acknowledge the tentative nature of its statements.

Possible misunderstandings or non-sequiturs from some of these points need to be guarded against, and I would like to select just three which call for further elucidation and comment.

1. The link between theology and the totality of human experience and knowledge should not be interpreted in a way which confuses, for teachers or for pupils, what is distinctive about theology, namely, that it is a speaking about God. If theology provides a language of 'enabling', as John Coulson has suggested on page 125, and if teachers should be thought of as enablers as Jo Gibson specifically states, a view much to the fore in the paper by Peter Hastings and Geoffrey Turner, then it is essential that in the classroom pupils are helped to see how theological language, offensive as it may appear to many, may provide a means of interpreting experience. If this is not made clear then the pupil is not equipped to make any bridge-building between the insights of theology and his or her own insights. The distinction between the what-has-happened of experience and the vocabulary in which it is dressed, to which John Kent draws attention on pages 115f., is crucial. Theology provides a unique explicit vocabulary: this is its purpose and raison d'etre.

2. Several contributors draw attention to the way in which theology should be seen as a searching. Its dynamic nature is thus assured and in a way which can render it significant and relevant to those who cannot

accept dogmatic theological assertions. Over-emphasis on this concept can, however, ignore the equally important fact that theology is to do with convictions and certainties both as regards what it expresses and the experience of those who express it however tentative its actual language is acknowledged to be. The only way in which justice can be done to both the aspect of open enquiry and of deep certainty is by gladly acknowledging that theology is controversial to its very roots and allowing pupils to know this, inviting them to think for themselves about it in agreement or disagreement.

In this way the commitment of the teacher and the commitment of the school as a whole if it explicitly seeks to be a Christian community can be made available to pupils without fear of dogmatically assuming their assent. In this way the tremendous benefits of a monastic environment, such as that found in Timothy Wright's school, can be utilized without influencing pupils in an undue manner, or arousing claustrophobic feeling amongst them. This would also make it proper for Simon Clements to bring the community of his comprehensive school together for worship, the desirability of which he considers on page 32. If this is to be done with educational propriety, there are, however, two requirements. Firstly, it must be made clear that attendance at worship assemblies requires an educational commitment to seek greater understanding of religion by experiencing something of a religious environment, rather than religious commitment on the part of the pupils involved. Secondly, there is an essential requirement that pupils should be encouraged to engage in positive reflection for themselves. This is paralleled by the way in which theology implies an educational but not necessarily a religious engagement. Although the latter may enhance the former – indeed many would argue that there is a limit beyond which theology cannot be understood without a religious conviction – this does not invalidate the point that the beginnings of theological reflection are accessible to the theologically uncommitted. Indeed, this is the way in which those to whom theological language means nothing may, perhaps, be enabled to discover its relevance.

The warning which John Kent voices against a 'revised fundamentalism' must be taken seriously but not by lapsing into some equally dogmatic form of relativism nor by playing down the challenge and the scandal of theological affirmations. The purpose both of teaching and of the total school community must be seen to be not to gain consensus to what is taught or the philosophy guiding its communal life but to stimulate real critical and thoughtful enquiry.

3. An awareness of the obstacles to theological understanding presented by the secular society in which children grow up, together

with the immaturity of their minds and limited experience, should not diminish but rather increase efforts to teach theology even to young children. Because of the difficulties, greater professionalism is called for so that the school can help to make up for the possible deficiencies of the home environment and the total cultural thought-forms which are imbibed.

Although the book is concerned with theology at 16+ a number of writers give the impression that theology really cannot be begun at much younger an age. This assumption needs to be challenged, not least because it runs counter to the way in which education should be seen as 'the continuous thread of learning, the seamless web' to quote Simon Clements (page 26). Many of the difficulties of teaching theology at 16+ stem from the fact that so much elementary ground has to be covered through the lack of any theology at infant, junior and lower secondary ages. Jo Gibson gives an example of the kind of understanding concerning 'the concept that truth is not always empirical, and that myths are not always necessarily intended as alternatives to a scientific interpretation of the world' which is quite capable of being appreciated by young children if in fact they are helped to see it. In a recent Farmington Discussion Paper, entitled *Religion and the Intellectual Capacities of Young Children*, Dora Ainsworth argues persuasively for theology at infant level, and a quotation she cites from Jerome Brunner deserves to be taken seriously:

> . . .any subject can be taught effectively in some intellectually honest form to any child at any stage of development. . . No evidence exists to contradict this hypothesis. Considerable evidence is being amassed that supports it.

There is also impressive evidence that failure to introduce concepts to children at an early age seriously retards later development of understanding. I suspect that adolescents will only be able to make valid judgments if earlier on in their schooling they have been given an opportunity to develop an inherent capacity for so doing. Furthermore, I would challenge the view presented by two or three contributors that religion is itself peculiarly an adult activity. In certain respects young children may be better equipped by virtue of their openness than some adults to receive religious insights. A book such as *Mister God, This is Anna* suggests it is possible seriously to underestimate the capacities of children. If they generally cannot articulate religious experience in a sophisticated way, perhaps this is because of the absence of education in theology.

To conclude with a case for theology even at 5+ is to underline in the manner of a three-line whip the necessity for it at 16+. Theology is a life-long enterprise, as it seeks paradoxically to hold together deep certainty with awareness of human inadequacy of comprehension: the expression in words of the inexpressible.